OXFORD
COLLEGE ARMS

British History in Oxford's Shields

JOHN TEPPER MARLIN, PhD
WITH HERALDIC ARTIST LEE LUMBLEY

BOISSEVAIN BOOKS, LLC
Washington, D.C. ▪ East Hampton, New York ▪ Vero Beach, Florida

End Notes, Bibliography, and Art/Photo Credits are posted on
TheOxfordPursuivant.blogspot.com blogsite, at https://bit.ly/2MTACMI.

Library of Congress Control Number: 2007012345

Published by Boissevain Books, LLC
Washington, D.C. ▪ East Hampton, New York ▪ Vero Beach, Florida
info@boissevainbooks.com
www.boissevainbooks.com

ISBN: 978-0-9845232-3-8

Edition 2019 20 19 18 17 16 15 14 13 12 11 10 9 8 7 6 5 4

Printed by IngramSpark
La Vergne, TN, USA
ingramsparksupport@ingramcontent.com

CONTENTS

PREFACE

BY RICHARD LOFTHOUSE

The original coat of arms was a cloak worn over a suit of armour to identify a medieval knight. Who'd have guessed that coats of arms would flourish right into modernity and even without arms? John Tepper Marlin, heraldry maven and former chief economist for New York City, brought this remarkable subject to my attention in 2015.

The resulting, fabulous essay in the Michaelmas issue of *Oxford Today* noted that of the 38 recognized Oxford colleges that survive today, fully 13 came into being in the past century, most of them post-1945.

The question we asked ourselves was why these recent colleges have coats of arms, when by all rights they needn't have bothered. The short answer is that inter-college sport demands identity. The colour and air of pageantry of coats of arms are rather well-suited to this task.

But what John did was to identify some stripes. St Anne's, St Antony's, St Catherine's, St Cross, and St Peter's all played safe and plumped for the arms of saints, or the sainted Field Marshal Plumer (St Anne's) or the holy cross for which the nearby church and road were named (St Cross). Kellogg, Harris Manchester, Linacre, and Green Templeton were more daring, their freely invented arms featuring the college mission.

My personal favourite is Wolfson, unique among the moderns by being the arms of the founder only, thus emulating the medieval tradition but for Sir Isaac Wolfson, the son of an immigrant to Glasgow from Bialystock, self-made rich by a mail order catalogue business. The first President, intellectual historian Sir Isaiah Berlin, was also an immigrant, from Latvia, and the Wolfson coat of arms is my favourite for its counterchanged pears, representing the fruits of labour. Oxford's most 'un-Oxford' college, having identified itself thus, confirmed a tradition while injecting it with new life, something that Oxford is pretty good at.

John has successfully interrogated the otherwise peculiar language of heraldry, providing an indispensable heraldic glossary at the end. The book in front of you is a big ripe pear full of juicy details about college coats of arms, the understanding of which (I'd wager) is generally poor. It deserves to be enjoyed by the widest audience, as well as carefully stored for reference.

October 2018

Dr Richard Lofthouse is the editor of QUAD, formerly Oxford Today,
the alumni magazine of the University of Oxford.

UNIVERSITY OF OXFORD

Highlights

- The Oxford arms feature the Bible (learning and piety) and crowns (royal favour).
- Teaching at Oxford is said to have been recorded in 1096; only Bologna is older.
- Students fleeing an Oxford town mob that lynched three students in 1209 created Cambridge University.
- The walls of the halls and colleges were designed, in part, to protect gown from town.

Arms, Blazon *Azure on a Book open proper garnished Or on the dexter side seven Seals of the last between three open Crowns of the second the words DOMINUS ILLUMINATIO MEA.* (The *blazon* is the formal record in words of a coat of arms. It follows certain rules, one of which is not to use punctuation, which was seen then as a common source of error. For explanation of terms in a blazon, refer to the Heraldic Glossary at the end of the book.)

Arms, Origin Henry III granted the University a royal charter in 1248 but the shield dates back only to about (*circa*, often abbreviated as c) 1400. Its origins and reasons for selection from many other once-prevalent forms of the shield are unclear.

Arms, Meaning The center of the Oxford coat of arms is the Bible (the words from Psalm 27 are translated "The Lord is my light"), a symbol of both *learning* and *religious piety*. The three crowns reference the patronage of kings. So the threefold message of the shield is: "Oxford is learned. Oxford is pious. Oxford has the protection of the Crown." Cambridge University's coat of arms also shows a Bible and signs of royal patronage, but its Bible is closed and on its side. Oxford's Bible, however, is open, ready for anyone to read.

Chancellor Since 1201 (or maybe before), Oxford University has been led by a Chancellor, whose role has now become akin to the chair of

the board. Since 2003, Oxford's Chancellor is Rt Hon Baron Patten of Barnes CH, who became a life peer in 2005. Christopher Patten was the first in his family to go to university, his father having been a jazz drummer. From St Benedict's School in Ealing, Patten won a scholarship to Balliol College, where he read Modern History. After graduation, he went on a Coolidge Traveling Scholarship to the United States. He visited the South in mid-1965, as Martin Luther King was marching toward Montgomery, Alabama for the Voting Rights Act. He did "oppo" research for John Lindsay's campaign for Mayor of New York City, covering conservative William F. Buckley, Jr. Though Buckley lost, he raised issues that still resonate. From his vivid experiences, Patten brought new ideas to London's Conservative Central Office, and he was made the Conservative Party's director of research. Elected a Member of Parliament, he became Secretary of State for the Environment, and then Chairman of the Conservative Party under Margaret Thatcher and John Major.

He gets credit for four consecutive Conservative victories, especially the closest win, in 1992. In 1992–97 he was famously the last British Governor of Hong Kong, and then a European Commissioner. He

was in 2011–2014 Chairman of the BBC Trust. As Chancellor, he has championed investment in the humanities ("because we're human") in an era when gifts and grants flow toward medical, scientific, and professional research and education. He has been married since 1971 to Lavender Thornton.

Vice Chancellor After an unbroken 800-year chain of male academic leaders, Oxford's top executive is now a woman, Professor Louise Mary Richardson. An expert on international security and terrorism, she was born in Tramore, County Waterford, Ireland, and was educated at Trinity College, Dublin (BA), UCLA (MA) and Harvard (PhD in Government). She was Principal of St. Andrews University and before that served as executive dean of the Radcliffe Institute for Advanced Study at Harvard. In an interview with *The*  *Guardian* about her nomination, Richardson said: "My parents did not go to college, most of my siblings did not go to college. The trajectory of my life has been made possible by education. So I am utterly committed to others having the same opportunity I have had." She has made one of her first priorities as Vice Chancellor to attract a higher percentage of students from lower-income communities—attempting to search more aggressively for the brightest students in schools that usually do not feed their graduates to Oxford, as opposed to the elite (typically boarding) schools, which account for more than 40 percent of current Oxford students.

Academic Standing The University of Oxford is ranked first in the world by THE World University Rankings (https://bit.ly/1Gd0ETp),

5th by QS (for Quacquarelli Symonds), and 7th by Academic Ranking of World Universities. The university operates the world's oldest university museum and largest university press. The Bodleian Library is one of the five greatest libraries in the world and is the largest academic library in Britain. Oxford's alumni include 29 Nobel laureates, 27 UK prime ministers, and many heads of state. As of 2017, 69 Nobel Prize winners and six Turing Award winners have studied, worked, or held visiting fellowships at Oxford, which is also the home of the Rhodes Scholarship. The Norrington Table (https://bit.ly/2KJGC5E) ranks the colleges on the aggregate performance of their senior undergraduates on their final examinations. The latest data provided under each college are the numbers released on August 20, 2018; they are subject to small revisions.

Head of the River, Bumps Since the Isis (the Thames as it passes Oxford) is narrow, boats cannot race side by side. The "Head of the River" races line up usually 12 eights, i.e., boats with eight oars plus a cox to steer, per division. A few boat-lengths are left between each boat. to bump the boat ahead. The winter bumps include about 130 boats and are called Torpids, after the lethargy of the season. The second set of bumps in the Trinity (Summer) term includes about 170 boats and are called Eights. Historical charts for each college as well as latest results for Torpids and Eights are at https://bit.ly/2I3FNGE.

Summer Eights before boathouses.

SPIRES OF OXFORD.

1,000 YEARS OF OXFORD HISTORY

Highlights

- 1066, Normans brought knives, forks and heraldry.
- 1096, Oxford's location on a crossroads made it a magnet for students.
- 1154, Henry II bore the first English royal arms; in 1167, he made Oxford a monopoly.
- 1334, Edward III blocked a plan for a third university; an Oxbridge duopoly lasted 500 years.
- 1441, Henry VI made the first royal grant to an Oxbridge college (King's, Cambridge).
- 1534, Henry VIII broke with Rome; in 1536 T. Cromwell started dissolving monasteries.
- 1642–49, Oxford colleges sheltered Charles I, but he was captured, tried, and beheaded.
- 1833–45, the Oxford Movement sucked up much Oxford energy; after it, reforms were rapid.
- 1878, the first women's college, Lady Margaret Hall was created.
- 1920, the Greek requirement for admission was dropped. 1960, Latin was dropped.
- 2017, the last Oxford Permanent Private Hall, St Benet's Hall, became coeducational.

11th–12th centuries—Oxford Is Second-Oldest University Oxford was an important Anglo-Saxon crossroads city long before it was the site of England's first university. The magnificent Bayeux tapestry shows that emblems were in use by the Anglo-Saxons as well as the Normans. When the fastidious Normans in 1066 defeated the Anglo-Saxons and brought knives (*canifes*) and forks (*fourchettes*) with them to England, along with enduring fancy names for cooked food, they also brought over their knights with their heraldry, and Oxford was one of the first places to adapt. The arrival of the Normans also kick-started an appreciation of the need for more education. So "evidence of teaching" in Oxford dates back to 1096, making Oxford the second-oldest university in continuous operation in the world, after Bologna, which began in 1088. Henry II made Oxford the only option for students in 1167 by forbidding English students from attending the University of Paris. He also created the first royal coat of arms in 1154. The first (1096–99) and second (1147–49) crusades had increased the popularity of heraldry. Under Henry III, heraldry developed its own language and classification system. Each landed family had emblems worn by knights, either as charges on an embroidered fabric over the knight's armour (coat of arms) or on a shield (shield of arms). A simpler version, a badge, was worn by servants. Another version was embossed on rings (seals) to be pressed into hot wax to identify and protect messages carried by heralds; hence the word heraldry.

13th century—First Colleges Oxford lost its monopoly in 1209, when a townswoman was killed and three Oxford University students were hanged in reprisal by a town lynch mob. In fear, many of the thousand-plus students and dons of the day fled east to the fens to form what became the University of Cambridge, the second-oldest British university. Oxford and Cambridge are often called "the ancient universities" and are referred to by the composite "Oxbridge". The strained relations with the town meant that abbots and bishops worried about their student monks, friars, and priests, and created halls to house and protect them. The first recorded hall was Blackfriars, founded in 1221 by Dominican monks, sent by St Dominic himself just before his death. Blackfriars would today be the oldest surviving hall . . . but after the Reformation the Dominicans stayed away from Oxford for four centuries. University College ("Univ") was founded by William of Durham in 1249. Balliol College was founded by Baron John de Balliol in 1255. Merton College was founded by Walter de Merton, a Lord Chancellor of England and afterwards Bishop of Rochester, in 1264. Merton is thus the third-oldest college but was the first to have a set of college regulations. Merton's structure became a model for other Oxbridge colleges. Students around this time associated on the basis of geographical origins, into southerners (English people south of the River Trent, and the Irish, Welsh, and Cornish)

and northerners (English people north of the river plus the Scots). Six of the once-more-numerous religious halls remain, distinguished from the colleges by their close ties to Catholic orders (Blackfriars, Campion Hall, and St Benet's) or to Protestant denominations or movements (Regent's Park College, St Stephen's House, and Wycliffe Hall). The other surviving halls have all become one of the 38 full colleges of the University. Heraldry, meanwhile, was growing apace, and the Falkirk Rolls, prepared soon after the 1298 Battle of Falkirk, near Edinburgh, include all of the major tinctures, metals and furs (see Heraldic Glossary at the end of the book), and many of the most-used charges. Edward I won this battle decisively, but Scotland won the war.

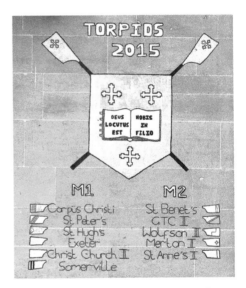

Chalked on the wall of Mansfield College.

14th century—Oxbridge Duopoly Oxbridge students gravitated toward structured college living, which offered a better quality of life than the halls, but not good enough for some. In 1333, a group of dissatisfied Oxford scholars set out to found a third university in Stamford, Lincolnshire. However, both Oxford and Cambridge protested and Edward III blocked the plan and in 1334 gave Oxbridge a duopoly that lasted nearly 500 years. This blanket of patronage encouraged creation of new colleges, i.e.,

Exeter, Oriel, The Queen's College, Canterbury (later absorbed into Christ Church), and New College. But in mid-century (1348–50) Britain joined Europe in being devastated by the Black Death, the world's worst-ever disaster, killing one-third to two-thirds of the populations of European nations, and an estimated one-fifth of the world's population. In this tragic environment, superstitions abounded, contributing on St Scholastica's Day 1355 to some more Oxford town-gown riots. Several Oxford students died again, prompting the Church to give the University privileges over the town that endured for half a millennium. During this century the seeds of the Reformation were planted in Oxford by John Wyclif, who questioned the wealth of the church and even the Pope's authority. He and his Oxford followers, the so-called Lollards, prepared a good first vernacular English translation of the Bible. Martin Luther was influenced by them and reprinted Wyclif's book *Trialogus*. Henry VIII later found Wyclif's thinking well-suited to explaining his break with Rome.

15th century More Oxford colleges were founded: Lincoln, All Souls, and Magdalen, despite the continuing need to adjust to the huge social dislocation caused by the Black Death and subsequent plagues. It took 200 years for the world's population to recover to what it was before 1348. In 1411, Thomas Arundel, Archbishop of Canterbury, an Oriel College man who spoke out against Lollardism, is an early example of bishops combining vertically (*impaling*) their personal arms with the permanent arms of their "Sees", i.e., the multi-parish regions overseen by the bishop. This is seen, for example, in the Brasenose, Corpus Christi and Lincoln College arms, where its use is questioned by heralds. After Arundel's death in 1414, the Archbishops of Canterbury continue to be Oxford men, often involved in the Oxford colleges—Chichele, Stafford, Kemp, Bourchier, Morton, Deane, Warham. The first royal heraldic position in England was created in 1420, when Henry V

created the Garter King of Arms, a uniquely English position. Henry VI granted arms to King's College, Cambridge in 1441 and Eton College in 1449, England's earliest recorded grants of academic heraldry. Richard III incorporated the College of Arms in 1484 as a corporate body based in London and consisting of the professional pursuivants, heralds, and kings of arms who are delegated heraldic authority by the British monarch. The English Law of Arms derives the right to grant arms from *due authority*, i.e., the Monarch or State; this authority in England and Wales is delegated to the College of Arms. The College survives today, one of the few remaining government heraldic authorities in Europe.

16th century The availability of the vernacular Bible and the questioning of the Pope's authority greatly influenced Oxford and emboldened Henry VIII to challenge Rome. Not having had a male heir with Catherine of Aragon, Henry VIII sought to annul their marriage in 1527. It was a bad year to ask Pope Clement VII for clemency; it was the year the Holy Roman Emperor Charles V sacked Rome. The weak Pope tried to please France by rejecting Henry VIII's request for an annulment; the standoff led to impatient Henry's break with Rome in 1534. Archbishop Thomas More and Bishop John Fisher were executed the next year for refusing to accept the supremacy of the King. Oxford lost lands, income, and influence. After Oxford's Archbishop Warham resigned when Henry VIII married Anne Boleyn, the next Archbishops of Canterbury, except for Reginald Pole under Mary I, were Cambridge men—Cranmer, Parker, Grindal, Whitgift, and Bancroft. In 1536, Thomas Cromwell started dissolving the monasteries, including six monastic colleges at Oxford and Cambridge. Henry VIII died in 1547, succeeded by the sickly nine-year-old Edward VI, who was controlled by Protestant courtiers. Edward died six years later, and his courtiers plotted to bypass Mary, daughter of Henry and Catherine, by installing Jane Grey (the "nine-day queen"). Their plan didn't stick, Jane was deposed and she was in due course executed. Mary I, called Mary Tudor to distinguish her from Mary Queen of Scots, tried to reestablish Catholicism. The last Catholic Archbishop of Canterbury, Reginald Pole, served in 1556–58. Mary I executed 280 Protestant religious leaders for heresy-treason, three of them in Oxford in front of Balliol College, all Cambridge men including Archbishop Cranmer. It was a dangerous period for the clergy, but five of the six dissolved Oxford and Cambridge colleges were refounded. They included, in 1555, Trinity and St John's on the land where Durham College had stood. Queen Elizabeth I's long reign (1558–1603) fostered a flowering of the arts and an uneasy standoff between Catholics, Anglicans and Protestant dissenters. Catholic scholars from Oxford fled to continental Europe, settling especially at the University of Douai.The method of teaching at Oxford was transformed from medieval scholasticism to Renaissance education, but morale and reputation were low. Only one college was founded during Elizabeth's reign, In 1573 the University of Cambridge was granted arms and the following year the arms of the University of Oxford and its colleges were recorded in a "Visitation" by a herald from the College of Arms.

Sign on the wall at the Eagle & Child, St Giles, Oxford.

17th century The dividing line at Oxford and Cambridge between their "old" colleges and "new" colleges is the death of Elizabeth I in 1603. With the accession of James I of England,

the simmering religious unrest boiled again. James I of England had ruled Scotland for a long time as James VI, where he favored the Catholic and Anglican bishops over the unpredictably democratic Presbyterians and other Protestant dissenters. When the two crowns were merged in his person and James I came to England, he paid lip service to Elizabethan laws against Catholics (which made Catholics unhappy), while informally giving Catholics some leeway (which made the dissenters unhappy). When his son Charles I became king in 1625, the Puritans were ready to resist the regime. Parliament organized a New Model Army (based on talent, not nobility), with two Cambridge men in charge—Yorkshireman Sir Thomas Lord Fairfax (cousin of the Fairfax celebrated at Gilling Castle where I was a pupil for a year) as Commander-in-Chief and Oliver Cromwell commanding the "Ironsides", lightly armed cavalry. After the well-drilled Parliamentarians defeated Royalist troops at Naseby in 1645, Charles I retreated to Oxford, where the University was reliably Royalist. As the Civil War continued (1642–1649), the colleges donated their silver collections to Charles I to pay for his soldiers, while Oxford's townspeople sided with the Parliamentarians. General Fairfax invaded Oxford and captured Charles I, who was tried by Parliament, sentenced to death, and beheaded. He was the only reigning monarch executed in England—no subsequent British monarch has gone on about the monarch's divine rights. Oliver Cromwell and Parliament ruled for a while, but when Cromwell died, public support for the lugubrious Puritans had faded. Charles II came in with the Restoration, maintaining the supremacy of the Anglican religion. However, his brother and heir James (later James II) worried many Britons when it was revealed that he was a Catholic. James II ruled at first with a benevolent spirit. But a couple of rebellions made him hostile and he began to lose support from his own Anglican Church. One thing he did, for example, was reserve Magdalen College, Oxford for Roman Catholics. Protestants of all stripes

hunted for an alternative king. They found one in the Netherlands, William III of Orange, married to James II's daughter Mary. Another schoolboy-familiar date, 1688, was the year of the "Glorious Revolution," when Parliament bloodlessly deposed James II and crowned William and Mary, preserving the form of the succession while changing its implications. Oxford, always central to the life of England, shared in every heartbeat of these developments. In 1636, its statutes were overhauled for the better by William Laud, Oxford's Chancellor and the Archbishop of Canterbury. Laud's work endured for more than 300 years, and his framework helped make the Oxford University Press and the Bodleian Library great Oxford assets. Science and philosophy, meanwhile, flourished in Oxford—the Oxford Philosophical Club met in the home of Wadham's Warden John Wilkins and became the nucleus of the science-focused Royal Society, founded 1660.

18th century The century was one of slow building of the foundations of the industrial revolution and a spiritual awakening, after the debilitating civil wars of the previous centuries. A. L. Rowse's book *Oxford in the History of the Nation* (1975) calls the century "An Age of Security". The Glorious Revolution put an end to violent religious civil wars. Some of the great buildings in Oxford went up at that time and a huge cast of world-famous people would spend time at Oxford. The only new college founded at Oxford was Worcester, a refounding of Gloucester Hall, but the existing colleges were seriously improving their buildings and engaging in social and religious experiments. Oxford University during this period had about 2,000 Fellows and students, almost all headed for the ministry, where the best-educated people were expected to serve. The curriculum was narrow and traditional. Of the many famed scientific thinkers, and writers, and doers who were at Oxford during the century, Rowse reserves his highest praise for John Wesley, founder of the Methodist Church. "[T]o be the founder of a world-church as John Wesley was—no Oxford man has ever accomplished more, and perhaps only [John Henry] Newman anything comparable." Big cities were growing fast—the size of

Aerial view of Oxford looking north. Christ Church to the left, then Corpus Christi College, Merton College, the Botanic Garden, and Magdalen College. Compare this with the illustrated view of Oxford looking northeast on pages 110–111.

London almost doubled in the century to one million residents, even though infant mortality was high. For every 1,000 children born in early-18th-century London, almost 500 died before they were two years old. Education was not widely available, but boys from well-off English and Scottish families had excellent schools to choose from, providing a steady flow to Oxford. Some girls also went to school, but were taught domestic skills like embroidery or music. English heraldry was in decline, as an increasing number of the newly wealthy designed coats of arms for themselves and just adopted them. The College of Arms was at a low point, with appointments not always based on what candidates knew about heraldry. The office of Clarenceux King of Arms, for example, the second-highest office in the College of Arms, was filled by an architect with no previous heraldic experience. No new grants of arms were made for several years in the early 1700s and annual new grants rose slowly, from 14 in 1747, to 40 in 1784, and just twice that a century later. The growth came from an increasing geographical spread in grantees and greater public interest in heraldry as the Romantic movement in art and literature venerated the medieval period.

19th century Oxford's vistas opened. Its role in nurturing and disseminating literature, religion, politics and science greatly expanded. The University attempted to recognize the growth of knowledge by separating honour schools for different subjects starting in 1802, with Mathematics and *Literae Humaniores* (Greats or Classics). Oxford's curriculum lagged the needs of its students. Sir Spencer Walpole, a senior government official who did not attend university, said that was the norm in many surprising vocations: "Few medical men, few solicitors, few persons intended for commerce or trade, ever dreamed of passing through a university career." Walpole was in awe of what Oxford did for its students, by providing them with a meeting place to educate one another:

> If the average undergraduate carried from University little or no learning [. . .] of any service to him, he carried from it a knowledge of men and respect for his fellows and himself, a reverence for the past, a code of honour for the present, which could not but be serviceable.

During the century, Oxford became more tolerant of dissenters, and less focused on training students for the Anglican ministry. It was Catholic bishops who discouraged their members from attending Oxford, even though the Oxford Movement (1833–1845) led to the conversion of Anglican John Henry Newman (Trinity, Oxford undergraduate, Oriel Fellow) to Catholicism. After that, the intensity of religious debate subsided and Oxford got busy updating itself. In 1866, membership in the Church of England was no longer required (as it had been since Elizabeth I) to receive the BA degree, and from 1871 Nonconformists were permitted to receive the MA. Of students who matriculated at Oxford in 1840, 59 percent became Anglican clergy. Thirty years later, the figure fell to 42 percent. The rise of organized sport, especially rowing and rugby, was a distinctive Oxbridge feature in the late 19th century, influenced by the growth in sports at the elite schools that fed into Oxford. Two parliamentary commissions in 1852 issued a program for Oxford reforms, with Archibald Campbell Tait, former headmaster of Rugby School, lauding the German-Scottish model, centered on the professors. The program called for such reforms as:

- Higher pay for professional staff and an expanded curriculum..

- An easier path to admission for less wealthy students (written entrance exams were introduced to base admissions on merit), undergraduate scholarships open to all Britons, and graduate fellowships open to all members of the University, not just to those planning to go into the ministry.

- Permission for students to save money by living in the town (in "digs") instead of in a college.

These recommendations were acted on. The university extension movement in the 1870s is a direct outgrowth of the work of the reformers. In 1878, Arthur Johnson delivered an "Oxford Extension Lecture". The university slowly began to open itself to religious nonconformists and poorer men and women. Meanwhile, the professions (science, medicine, law) rose in importance in the curriculum. Schools of "Natural Sciences" and "Law, and Modern History" were added in 1853 and by 1872, the Law School was split off as "Jurisprudence", leaving "Modern History" as its own School. Theology became the sixth honour school. The influence of the reformed model of German universities reached Oxford via scholars such as Edward Bouverie Pusey and Benjamin Jowett (Balliol College).

19th–20th centuries—Education for Women
The first woman to pass exams that should have earned her a degree was Annie Mary Anne Henley in 1877. The first four women's colleges at Oxford were established through the efforts of the Association for Promoting the Higher Education of Women, proposed by the enlightened first Warden of Keble, John Talbot. Lady Margaret Hall (1878) for Anglican women was followed by Somerville College (1879) for dissenters. The first students attended lectures in rooms above a baker's shop. St Hugh's (1886) and St Hilda's (1893) followed. The university passed a statute in 1875 allowing undergraduate examinations, which briefly in the early 1900s qualified the so-called "steamboat ladies" to cross the Irish Sea to obtain degrees from the University of Dublin. The University admitted women to degree study in 1920. In 1927–57 the University limited female students to one-quarter the number of men. A fifth women's college was founded, St Anne's (1952), which had been operating for years before without college status. Not until 1959 were the women's colleges given full collegiate status.

Barely a quarter-century after St Anne's became the fifth women's college, all of the women's colleges began to go coeducational, starting with LMH and St Anne's in 1979 and ending with St Hilda's in 2008. In 1974, Brasenose, Hertford, Jesus, St Catherine's and Wadham were the first men's colleges to admit women. The majority of men's colleges started accepting female students in 1979, with Oriel the last in 1985. Not until 2017 did St Benet's Hall become the last Permanent Private Hall to embrace coeducation. In 1988, 40 percent of undergraduates at Oxford were female; in 2016, 45 percent of students, and 47 percent of undergraduates, were female. The graduate colleges admitted women much earlier; female medical students, as early as 1916. Most of Oxford's graduate colleges were coeducational from the start, with the exception of St Antony's, which began to accept women only in 1962. In 2018, for the first time, women at Oxford outnumbered men.

20th century Religious requirements at Oxford, such as compulsory daily worship, continued to be loosened and ancient theological bequests were redirected to serve newer subjects of study. Knowledge of Ancient Greek was dropped in 1920 as a requirement for admission. Even Latin was toppled in 1960. The University of Oxford began to award doctorates in the first third of the century and the first Oxford DPhil in mathematics was

Enthusiastic readers of Oxford College Arms at the Old Parsonage, April 2019.

awarded in 1921. Many distinguished Continental scholars displaced by Nazi and Soviet persecution relocated to Oxford, adding to the University's academic strength.

College arms on plates, displayed in Oxford shop window.

21st century In 2018, Oxford University is made up of 38 colleges, six Permanent Private Halls (PPHs) and four academic divisions—Humanities, Social Sciences, Mathematical, Physical and Life Sciences, and Medical Science. A fifth, nonacademic, division includes Gardens, Libraries, And Museums (GLAM). The interesting GLAM Division is led by Professor Anne Trefethen https://www.admin.ox.ac.uk/glam/. University Administration and Services serves as the staff office of the University—https://www.admin.ox.ac.uk/—headed by the Registrar, who from September 2018 is Gill Aitken, formerly General Counsel at HM Revenue and Customs.

The colleges are self-governing institutions. They provide undergraduates with weekly tutorials. Tutorials are supported by the academic divisions, which offer classes, lectures, seminars, and laboratory work. Some graduate teaching includes departmental tutorials. While the six Permanent Private Halls retain some affiliation with religious bodies, they do not require applicants for admission to subscribe to any faith or movement.

ALL SOULS COLLEGE

Highlights

- Founded 1438 by Archbishop of Canterbury under Henry VI.
- Only college at Oxford where all members are Fellows.
- Every hundred years, they lasciviously hunt for a mallard.
- Famed Fellows include T. E. Lawrence and Christopher Wren.

Arms, Blazon *Or a Chevron between three Cinquefoils pierced Gules.* (Consult "Arms, Meaning" below for explanation of the *charges,* and the Glossary at the end of this book to translate any terms that are not made clear by comparing the coat of arms with the blazon.)

Arms, Origin Ancient. Predates the College of Arms, founded in 1484. The College of Arms grandfathered arms that were in existence before it was created. The arms did not have to be "granted" to be authoritative. However, the College of Arms reserved the right to "Visit" arms-bearing families and institutions, and to review their right to bear their arms.

Arms, Nominee The founder, Henry Chichele, born 1362, was Archbishop of Canterbury from 1414 till his death in 1441.

Arms, Meaning The upside-down V (*chevron*) is a charge that represents a sheltering rafter, a roof. The three pierced five-leaf flowers (*cinquefoils*), from Chichele's arms, signify hope and joy. A chevron appears in the arms of 13 Oxford colleges.

Founded 1438, the College of All Souls of the Faithful Departed is the ninth-oldest college at Oxford. It was planned in 1436 by Archbishop Chichele of Canterbury. Henry VI was added as co-founder by the time its foundation stone was laid on 10 February 1438. Five years later, its first buildings were complete and it received its statutes, modeled on those of New College.

Where to See Arms

The arms appear on the wrought-iron gates of the college on Catte Street opposite the Radcliffe Camera, and in front of the college on High Street.

15th century—Archbishop Chichele (1362–1441). Henry Chichele, whose arms are featured on the All Souls shield, was a man of great influence. He attended Winchester and New College, and believed in a close alliance of Church and State. He favored a war with France, taking the northern, Burgundian side of the French civil war, in support of Pope Urban VI. Their opponents were the Armagnacs, the House of Orléans and the Avignon Pope Clement VI. He showed up at the battle of Agincourt in 1415 to make sure God was on the side of the King. Chichele negotiated Henry V's marriage to Princess Catherine of Valois and in 1421 crowned her Queen of England. Later, he christened her son, the future Henry VI. In those days, archbishops were wealthy, and Chichele was a generous benefactor, supporting poor students at Oxford with funds kept in "Chichele's Chest". He also gave money to New College and the Cistercian College of St Bernard, which after its dissolution under Henry VIII became

Archbishop Henry Chichele, Founder.

St John's College. His greatest legacy to Oxford was funding All Souls, allowing a Warden and 40 Fellows to spend their time in prayer and study. He is honored by Oxford's chair of modern history being named the "Chichele Professorship".

15th century—The Lord Mallard (1437–)

With high admission standards, requiring candidates to have a first-class degree, All Souls Fellows have excelled at study, although piety has not been as much on their agenda as Archbishop Chichele might have liked. Once per century since its foundation, most recently on 14 January 2001, the Fellows engage in a Roman bacchanalia. After a great feast, they have paraded around the College with flaming torches, singing the bawdy *Mallard Song,* led by a "Lord Mallard" who is carried in a chair. The Fellows claim to seek a mallard that flew out of the college's foundations when newly constructed in 1437. A man precedes the Lord Mallard on foot, bearing a pole to which a mallard is tied—originally a live bird, a dead one in 1901, and a wooden one in 2001. The ceremony takes place in part on the rooftops. Warden Richard Astley (in office 1618–36), referred to it as "barbarously unbeseeming conduct". But it lives on and will presumably be repeated in 2101.

20th century—Warden Sparrow (1908–1992)

Another bird, John Sparrow (Winchester and New College) was head of house, Warden of All Souls in 1952–77. He had early publishing success, and was swept into All Souls as an Oxford wit. For example, he described his College as a "hotbed of cold feet". He became notorious with his exegesis in *Encounter* Magazine on the trial of D. H. Lawrence's *Lady Chatterley's Lover.* Sparrow averred that based on his close reading of the book, it was more pornographic than the judges could comprehend and should under the laws of the time have been found guilty. *The Guardian* reported 50 years later:

In 1959, . . . Parliament passed a new Obscene Publications Act . . . [T]he attorney general, Reginald Manningham-Buller, in August 1960 [urged] prosecution of Penguin Books. [Part of the problem was the inexpensive price, which made it accessible to *hoi polloi.* The outcome was that the jury acquitted Penguin Books.] No other jury verdict in British history has had such a deep social impact. Over the next three months Penguin sold 3 million copies of the book . . . [T]he attempt to suppress a book through unsuccessful litigation served only to promote huge sales.

His article includes a soliloquy on a word traceable to 1555, referencing the Bulgarian Bogomils sect that believed creating children was a sin, and therefore urged forms of intercourse that avoided procreation. Meanwhile, Sparrow's high standards sadly meant that he never considered his major projects good enough to publish.

Famed Fellows All Souls admits selected graduates from among those who earned first-class degrees. Notable former Fellows include T. E. Lawrence, aka Lawrence of Arabia, who was an undergraduate at Jesus College, and architect Christopher Wren, who was an undergraduate at Wadham.

Current Head of House The Warden is Sir John Vickers, elected 2008. He was an undergraduate at Oriel College. He served as Chief Economist at the Bank of England and in 2010, he became Chair of the UK's Independent Commission on Banking. In May 2018 he expressed concern about the "dangerously high" leverage of banks.

Academic and Rowing Standing As a graduate college of Fellows, All Souls is not in the Norrington Table. It does not compete in Torpids and Eights Week.

BALLIOL COLLEGE

Highlights

- Founded 1263 as penance meted out to a claimant to the Scottish throne.
- Rival with Trinity at least since the 1690s.
- Was an early actor in encouraging the co-education of women students.
- Adam Smith studied here, as did three Prime Ministers.

Arms, Blazon *Azure a Lion rampant Argent crowned Or* (for Galloway) *impaling Gules an Orle Argent* (for Balliol).

Arms, Origin Ancient. Predates the College of Arms, founded in 1484. Recorded in the 1574 Oxford Visitation.

Arms, Nominees John, Fifth Baron de Balliol and (since 1850) his widow Dervorguilla, added to the arms impaled dexter.

Arms, Meaning Balliol College's rampant lion indicates Scottish royalty, which came from Alan Galloway, the father-in-law of the founder, the Fifth Baron of Bywell, John de Balliol. Lord de Balliol was a rival with Robert de Bruce for the throne of Scotland. Balliol founded the college at Oxford as penance imposed by the Prince Bishop of Durham, for disputing the Prince Bishop's authority in 1255. Balliol College was originally created as a home for 16 poor scholars. When de Balliol died in 1268, his widow, Lady Dervorguilla de Galloway, carried her late husband's heart with her in a case and carried out his wishes to complete the creation of the Oxford hall. Because the rampant lion indicates Scottish royalty, it is impaled dexter (right from the knight's perspective), the senior position, even though the wife is normally in the other position, sinister and secondary. The Fifth Baron Balliol's coat of arms is plain red (*gules*) except for the silver (*argent*) border of the shield interior to what would be a bordure (*orle*).

College Founded 1263, Statutes adopted 1282.

13th century—King John I (reigned 1292–1296). Two years after the death of his widowed mother Dervorguilla, her son became King of Scotland. The deaths of Alexander III (he fell off his horse) and his princess daughter, heiress to the throne, left the succession unclear and 13 contenders vied to become the next king. England's Edward I ("Longshanks"), recruited by the nobles to pick Scotland's king from the contenders, chose the Sixth Baron de Balliol. So he was crowned John I in 1292 on the Stone of Destiny at Scone, the last Scottish king to be so crowned. John I reigned for just four years, as he was caught between a battle of wills between the nobles and Longshanks. When Edward I demanded Scottish troops to fight Philip IV of France, John I was pressured in 1295 to sign an alliance with Philip IV against Edward. So began a long-running "Auld" Alliance between Scotland and France. Outraged at Scotland, Edward I came north in 1296 with an army. He sacked the border city of Berwick and crushed the Scots at the Battle of Dunbar. He brought back with him both King John I and the precious Stone of Destiny. The Stone was returned 700 years later, in 1996, but John was never returned. He was first imprisoned till 1299 in the Tower of London and was then exiled to Normandy. Edward I thus earned the name "Hammer of the Scots" while John I was called "Toom Tabard" (Empty Coat), i.e., a weak man. Stronger rebels stepped up in Scotland, led by William Wallace ("Braveheart") and Andrew

Moray. They defeated English troops at Stirling Bridge and waged an effective "secret war" (guerilla war) against Longshanks.

16th century—The Snell Dinner Balliol's Scottish connection has been celebrated annually since at least 1550, with a dinner on 25 November, the feast day of the College patron saint, martyr St Catherine of Alexandria, after whom St Catherine's College is named. This dinner honors John Snell, whose benefaction established scholarships for students from the University of Glasgow to study at Balliol. One such scholar was the great economist Adam Smith.

In front of Balliol, X marks the spot where the three Oxford Martyrs were burned.

16th century—Queen Mary's Martyrs Balliol College's Scottish affiliation takes on significance in light of the later martyrdom of three Anglican bishops under England's Mary I. The martyrs are memorialized on both sides of Balliol College's western corner. On the street opposite the Broad Street door of Balliol is a large cross, marking where the three bishops were burnt at the stake by Catholic Mary I ("Bloody Mary"), Henry VIII's eldest child. On the other side of the corner, on St Gile's, is the Martyrs Memorial, dedicated to the bishops' memory. During Mary I's reign, the Scots might still have been grieving over the execution by Queen Elizabeth of her Catholic older sister, Mary Queen of Scots, so the martyrdom

of the Church of England bishops might not have been universally mourned at Balliol. Of the three martyrs, greater credit is given to Archbishop Thomas Cranmer, a talented man who saw some merit in the accusations leveled against him, and bravely died for his faith anyway, than to Hugh Latimer and Nicholas Ridley, who never had doubts.

Martyrs' Memorial.

17th century on—The Feud A longstanding feud with Trinity College sometimes flares up in the Torpids and Summer Eights races on the Isis, in practical jokes played or songs sung (especially, by Balliol, the "Gordouli") outside the walls of the other college, and in mutterings about the other college in public places. The rivalry is first noted in the 1690s, when the President of Trinity, Ralph Bathurst, was reported to have thrown stones at Balliol's windows. Balliol may have shown its envy of the Trinity gardens in 1963, during this author's time at Trinity, when some enterprising Balliol undergraduates sought *Gartenraum* by turfing the floor of the Trinity Junior Common Room and transplanting a host of golden daffodils. Less innocently, Balliol ruffians vandalised Trinity's Senior Common Room pond, leading to the widely mourned deaths of all but one of the SCR fish.

19th century—Students Wage Secret War

Guerilla tactics were utilized by Balliol students to pillory their Master and dons in 1880. Seven Balliol undergraduates anonymously published *The Masque of B-ll--l*, a broadsheet of forty quatrains making light of their Fellows. Verses of this form are now known as Balliol rhymes. The best-known of these rhymes is the one on Benjamin Jowett:

> *First come I. My name is J-W-TT.*
> *There's no knowledge but I know it.*
> *I am Master of this College,*
> *What I don't know, Isn't knowledge.*

20th century—Admission of Women

Balliol was a relatively early mover on admission of women to equal status. Whereas for more than seven centuries, like all other male colleges at Oxford, it admitted men only, in 1967 Balliol provided the Holywell Manor site where Balliol and St Anne's undergraduates studied and were taught together. In 1973, Carol Clark was appointed a Balliol Tutorial Fellow, the first female so appointed at Oxford. In 1979, along with some other previously all-male colleges, Balliol accepted its first female students. In 2010, the college unveiled a sundial in the Garden Quad commemorating the 30th anniversary of the admission of women to the college, inscribed "About Time".

Current Head of House

The Master since 2012 is the first woman to hold the post, Dame Helen Ghosh, former Director General of the National Trust, Home Office Permanent Secretary, and alumna of St Hugh's and Hertford Colleges. Ghosh was appointed Private Secretary to the Minister for Environment and Housing in 1986–88, and was promoted to Head of the Housing Policy and Home Ownership Team in 1992. Three years later, she joined the Cabinet Office on loan, as Deputy Director of the Efficiency Unit. She later worked at the Department for Work and Pensions as Director of the Children's Group, with responsibility for child, child support, child poverty issues and the tax credit program. In 2001 she returned to the Cabinet Office and two years later became Director General for Corporate Services at HM Revenue and Customs.

Academic and Bumps Standing

The Norrington Table ranks Balliol 5th on the 2006–16 average, 8th in 2016, 11th in 2017, and 9th in 2018 (Trinity was one place behind, 10th). In Summer Eights 2018, Balliol's first men's eight made one bump and rose from 8th place to 7th. The first women's eight had one net negative bump, and so falling from 13th to 14th place. On points, Balliol stayed in 10th place on the river. The five crews netted six bumps, the 9th-best 2018 record.

BLACKFRIARS

- Oldest extant hall at Oxford, founded 1221; absent from Oxford 1536–1921.

- The black-and-white coat of arms matches the order's white tunic and black cloak.

- St Dominic founded his order to combat heresy; they became "the hounds of Heaven".

- Today, Blackfriars is a graduate center for students and a Dominican priory.

Arms, Blazon *Gyronny Sable and Argent a Cross flory counterchanged.*

Arms, Origin The arms are those of the Dominican Order, officially founded in France in 1216. Blackfriars was established five years later in Oxford.

Arms, Meaning The black-and-white Gyronny Cross references the black-on-white Dominican habit—a long white tunic, covered by a black cloak, cappa, or scapular. The black and white is commonly interpreted as heresy vs. truth, perhaps because the black cloak can be taken off. St Dominic's original mission was to counter heresy. The Cross flory, with a fleur-de-lys on the end of each limb of the cross, refers to St Dominic's plan to preach to the heretical Cathars of southern France.

13th century—Foundation The first thirteen Dominican friars were sent by the General Chapter in Bologna, headed by St Dominic, and arrived in Oxford on 15 August 1221, one week after the friar's death. Even then Oxford was seen as England's intellectual capital, probably because of Robert Grosseteste (1175–1253), who was Bishop of Lincoln and has been called the founder of the scientific method at Oxford. The first Blackfriars hall was built in Oxford's Jewish Quarter near today's Town Hall. A larger hall was erected in 1245 through a gift from the Countess of Oxford, expanding it to 90 friars. This is Oxford's oldest documented hall. The Dominicans were called the "Hounds" or "Watchdogs" of Heaven in part because of their passion for refuting false doctrine. They were chosen along with the Franciscans by Gregory IX (Pope 1227–41) to judge heresy, and the aggressiveness of the Inquisitions was most pronounced in Spain. There were no papal inquisitions in England. Another explanation for nicknaming the Dominicans "hounds" is that St Dominic's mother had a dream while pregnant that a dog leaped out from her with a torch to set the world on fire. The word "Dominican" also sounds like the Latin "Domini" (Lord) plus "Canis" (Dog).

16th century Like other monastic houses in Oxford, Blackfriars came into conflict with Wyclif's Lollards and other critics of Church wealth and hierarchy. The Lollard criticisms were deployed by Henry VIII in his rationale for dissolving the monasteries. Having lost their home in Oxford, the Dominicans did not return for nearly four more centuries.

20th century Although the Benedictines and Jesuits returned to Oxford as soon as they could, in 1895–96, the Dominicans did not come back to found a third priory until 1921, under the leadership of Fr. Bede Jarrett. Blackfriars fully reopened in 1929.

Blackfriars coat of arms on a sweater.

21st century Blackfriars uniquely serves three functions—as a hall for students, a Priory for about twenty Dominican friars and a Study Centre for theology in the tradition of St Thomas Aquinas. It admits men and women of any faith for Oxford undergraduate degrees in theology schools, in Philosophy, Politics and Economics; and admits graduate students in many subjects.

Current Head of House The current Regent of both the Hall and Studium is Very Rev Dr Simon Gaine OP. The prior is Very Rev David Goodill OP.

Academic and Bumps Standing. The Norrington Table did not rank Blackfriars in 2017. In 2018, Blackfriars was ranked 1st of the six PPHs. Its score would have put it in 2nd place after St John's but the PPHs have small numbers of exam-takers and they are properly segregated from the colleges. Blackfriars did not compete in 2018 Summer Eights.

BRASENOSE COLLEGE

Highlights

- One of Oxford's most complicated coat of arms.
- The oldest college founded in part by a layman (lawyer).
- George Washington's ancestor Lawrence was a don here.

Arms, Blazon *Tierced in pale First Argent a Chevron Sable between three Roses Gules* (for Smyth) *Second Gules two Lions passant guardant Or on a Chief Azure Our Lady sitting with her Babe Crown and Scepter of the second* (for the see of Lincoln) *ensigned with a Mitre proper* (for Smyth) *Third Argent a Chevron between three Bugle Horns stringed Sable quartering Argent a Chevron between three Crosses crosslet Sable* (for Sutton).

Arms, Origin Ancient arms, predated the College of Arms.

Arms, Meaning The bishop's personal arms are on the left-hand (*dexter*) third of the shield, i.e., the arms of the Bishop of Lincoln, William Smyth of Lancashire. The red roses are for Lancaster. The permanent arms of the See of Lincoln (which at that time included Oxford) are in the middle third. They are the same arms as appear in the middle of the Lincoln College shield. The right-hand portion (*sinister*) represents the arms of Sir Richard Sutton of Macclesfield, Cheshire.

Arms, Issues (1) Use of the arms of a See on a college is questioned by heraldic authorities. Therefore the entire mitred middle pale, as used on all three tierced college shields, may be improper, though protected by their ancient usage. (2) Tiercing of arms produces a tiny version of Our Lady with Infant Jesus and sceptre, indecipherable unless liberties are taken with the usual proportions for a device "on a chief".

16th century—Founded In 1509, Brasenose College (usually known as BNC) was founded jointly by a lawyer and a bishop, on the site of Brasenose Hall, which got its name from the brass knocker on the front door. It was the first college to have a non-clerical founder. The college is associated with Cheshire and Lancashire, which are the county origins of its two founders. This link with the two counties was maintained until the latter half of the twentieth century.

17th century—Lawrence Washington, Inquisitor, then Heretic Brasenose was a hotbed of both Heretic-Hunting and Resistance. During the Reformation, it had Catholic sympathisers. During the English Civil War (Charles I vs. Cromwell) most of Brasenose favoured the Royalist side, but the College produced many clerics and generals on both sides. A BNC alumnus and don named Lawrence Washington became a Proctor, hunting down heretical (anti-royal) dons. When the tide turned to Cromwell's Interregnum, Washington (by then married) was in the fine Parish of Purleigh. He was replaced and given a much smaller parish. His status-conscious wife Amphyllis was appalled and moved out to live with her better-off uncle. Their two sons Lawrence Jr and John were packed off to Virginia to seek their fortune. Amphyllis would have been consoled to know that her great-great-grandson George Washington would become the Father of His Country. Lawrence Washington's coat of arms, inherited by George, became the flag of Washington, DC, and many (including the author) believe that the mullets and bars of the Washington arms were a decisive influence on the creation of the U.S. Stars and Stripes.

19th century—Oldest Boat Club The BNC's boat club is said to be the world's oldest, along with Jesus College, Oxford, against which it rowed for the title of Head of River in 1815. That was 14 years before the first Oxford-Cambridge boat race, from Iffley Lock to Mr King's Barge at Folly Bridge. Both crews rowed in eight-oared boats. Exeter and Christ Church were the next two colleges to join what became Torpids and Eights Week.

Current Head of House The Principal since 2015 is John Bowers QC, a British barrister and part-time judge. Born in Grimsby, he was educated at Clee Grammar School in Cleethorpes, and then read law at Lincoln College, Oxford. He was called to the Bar in 1979, took silk (became a Queen's Counsel) in 1998, and has been a deputy High Court Judge since 2010. He is an honorary professor at the University of Hull.

Academic and Bumps Standing Brasenose ranked 15th on the Norrington Table for the years 2006–2016. In 2016, 2017, and 2018 the college ranked a steady 7th among the colleges. Brasenose shares a boathouse with Exeter College (#5 in the main cluster). They both have coats of arms outside the boathouse doors, a red door for Exeter's and a black one for BNC. In 2018 Summer Eights, Brasenose filled five boats. The Brasenose first men's eight ranked 22nd at the start and was bumped every day, ending at 26th place out of 92 boats. The first women's eight was bumped only once, dropping from 29th to 30th place out of 79 boats. On points, BNC fell from 22nd to 26th place.

Brasenose College Old Quad.

CAMPION HALL

Highlights

- Arms are for martyred Jesuit priest Edmund Campion.

- Students are primarily graduates.

Arms, Blazon *Argent on a Cross Sable a Plate charged with a Wolf's Head erased of the second between in pale two Billets of the field that in chief charged with a Cinquefoil and that in base with a Saltire Gules and in fess as many plates each charged with a Campion flower leaved and slipped proper on a Chief also of the second two branches of Palm in saltire infiled with a Celestial Crown Or.* (Any unfamiliar terms can be consulted in the Glossary at the back of this book.)

Arms, Origin Granted 4 Nov 1935.

Arms, Meaning
The small saltire in the bottom arm of its ordinary sable cross may be taken to be the red St Patrick's cross, and references the Irish origin of the Jesuit missionaries sent from Dublin, who included the martyred Fr Edmund Campion. Other devices refer to Campion—a cross flanked with two campion flowers and with a wolf's head at its centre, this being a heraldic symbol of the Loyola family (*lobo* meaning wolf), of which a distinguished member, baptized Íñigo López and later known as Ignatius, founded the Jesuit

Order. The top arm of the sable cross includes a cinquefoil, which is often interpreted as signifying hope and joy. In chief are two crossed palm branches of victory and a gold crown of triumph, illustrating the Christian belief in the significance of dying for one's faith. Campion Hall's Latin motto (not shown) is *Veritatem facientes in Caritate* ("Doing the truth in love"); this captures the essence of the Hall.

Campion Hall.

19th–20th centuries Campion Hall was founded in 1896 by the Society of Jesus. This Roman Catholic order was created in 1540 to advance education, especially higher education. Jesuit missionaries from Dublin were successful evangelists at Oxford until Roman Catholics were banned from the University during 1581–1871 (i.e., from Elizabeth I to Victoria). Although accepted by the University in 1871–1895, Catholics were forbidden by their English bishops from attending, for fear they would be contaminated by Protestantism. The prohibition was relaxed in 1895, and the Ampleforth Benedictines were the first to come back, creating St Benet's Hall to help their monks gain Oxford degrees. The following year, Jesuit priest Fr Richard Clarke, alumnus of St. John's College, opened "Clarke's Hall", first based at St. Aloysius Church and then at 40 St Giles. He was the first Master, with four students. The second Master was Fr Pope; during his term the Hall was widely known as Pope's Hall.

21st century Campion Hall today provides a home for graduate studies built around the Jesuit community life, while accepting scholars from different traditions, secular and religious. Within the University, Campion Hall seeks to foster joy in learning, in the spirit of St Augustine. It had one undergraduate student in 2017–18 and nine graduate students.

Current Head of House The Master since 2013 is Revd James Hanvey, S.J. Born in Belfast, Northern Ireland, James gained his Oxford doctorate on the metaphysics of the doctrine of the Trinity. After serving as Headmaster of St Aloysius' College, Glasgow, he taught systematic theology at Heythrop College, University of London. He has also been a theological consultant to the Bishops of England and Wales. At the University of San Francisco he was the Lo Schiavo Professor of Catholic Social Thought. His recent writings include "Dignity, Person, Imago Trinitatis", in *Understanding Human Dignity* (ed. Christopher McCrudden, 2013) and "For the Life of the World" in *The Second Vatican Council* (ed. Gavin D'Costa and Emma Jane Harris, 2013).

Academic and Bumps Standing The Norrington Table did not rank Campion Hall in 2017 or 2018. Campion Hall did not compete in the 2018 Summer Eights.

CHRIST CHURCH

Highlights

- Arms are for Cardinal Wolsey, founder of the college, with Henry VIII.
- Largest college, produced 13 prime ministers.
- Lewis Carroll (Charles Dodgson), Author of *Alice in Wonderland,* taught here.
- Other alumni include John Locke, William Penn, John Wesley, W. H. Auden.

Arms, Blazon *Sable on a Cross engrailed Argent a Lion passant Gules between four Leopards' heads [caboshed] Azure on a Chief Or a Rose of the third seeded of the fifth barbed Vert between two Cornish Choughs proper* (for Wolsey).

Arms, Origin Henry VIII gave a dispensation from the Oxford colleges' having to obtain a grant from the College of Arms. This would apply especially to the college he considered his own.

Arms, Meaning The shield is a visual biography of the college's founder, Cardinal Thomas Wolsey, who worked for a young Henry VIII and was the leading churchman in England until the question of divorcing Catherine of Aragon came up and Wolsey was slow to take the King's side. Each device on the coat of arms is a reference to Wolsey's power. The engrailed cross was from the arms of the Earls of Suffolk. The lion passant guardant is for Pope Leo X, the red rose for Wolsey's Lancashire birthplace. The Cornish choughs with red feet and beaks are for Thomas à Becket. A commoner, Wolsey displayed his local power.

Founded in 1525 as "Cardinal College" by Cardinal Wolsey, his role was diminished when he opposed Henry VIII's divorcing Catherine in favor of Anne Boleyn. The miffed Henry VIII refounded the college first as "King Henry VIII College" and then in 1546 as Christ Church,

without the "College" suffix. Christ Church takes many students from Westminster School as well as Eton College.

Alumni Christ Church has produced 13 British Prime Ministers, considerably more than any other Oxford or Cambridge college. The two Oxford runners-up are Balliol and Trinity, with three each. Famed alumni besides Lewis Carroll include: John Locke, John Wesley, William Penn, and W. H. Auden. Of all these, only Carroll was a rower.

13th century—St Frideswide Christ Church is primarily a church, the only college that is also a cathedral, England's smallest. It never takes the suffix "college". Its links to the Anglican Church are extensive and it would have to be a Permanent Private Hall, except that Henry VIII gave the church the status of a college. It is the largest college at Oxford. Its Shrine of St Frideswide was built in 1289 in honor of an 8th century nun, Frideswide, patron saint of Oxford. The Cathedral was built in the 12th and 13th centuries, before the college was founded, and has Romanesque and Gothic architecture.

17th century—Civil War. During the Civil War, 1642–1646, Charles I headquartered himself at Christ Church. His army kept their cattle in the Great Quad and kept hay for the cattle in the Cathedral.

17th century–Tom Tower. The famous tower over the entrance to the college was designed by the architect Sir Christopher Wren in 1681–82. The bell in the tower is known as "Great Tom", and it chimes 101 times every evening at 9pm, once for each of the original 101 students of Christ Church.

17th century—Dr. John Fell (1625–1686) was Dean of Christ Church, where he created a "learned *imprimerie*" that in 1690 was handed over to the University and became the center of what became the Oxford University Press. Initially the Press published just one book every three years. Now it publishes 6,000 a year. Fell was the subject of satirical verse that became a popular nursery rhyme. One of John Fell's students, Tom Brown, was scheduled to be "sent down" for an infraction of the rules. Dr Fell offered a possible pardon if Brown could translate some Latin extemporaneously. Fell decided on an epigram (#32) by Martial, as follows: *Non amo te, Sabidi, nec possum dicere quare; / Hoc tantum possum dicere, non amo te.* Brown's brilliant (Dr Seuss-like) translation, switching the target to the Dean himself, is all that is remembered today about Tom Brown, who became a writer of national satire, or of Dr Fell, who became Bishop of Oxford:

> *I do not like thee, Doctor Fell,*
> *The reason why—I cannot tell;*
> *But this I know, and know full well,*
> *I do not like thee, Doctor Fell.*

In a rare moment of mercy, an appreciative Dr Fell granted Brown the promised pardon.

19th century—Lewis Carroll The author of the *Alice in Wonderland* books (real name Charles Lutwidge Dodgson), was a student and then lecturer at the college. His "Alice" books came from stories he told on punting trips with the Dean's teenaged daughter Alice, often with another don from Trinity.

21st century–Film Location The college has been used in the films of J.K. Rowling's Harry

Potter books, and *The Golden Compass*, based on Philip Pullman's *Northern Lights*. The dining halls at the University of Chicago and Cornell University are both reproductions of the vast Christ Church dining hall.

Christ Church Cathedral.

Current Head of House Since 2014 the 45th Dean of Christ Church is Martyn William Percy, an Anglican priest. Percy teaches in the Faculty of Theology and Religions, and is a fellow of the Saïd Business School. Educated at Merchant Taylors' School, Northwood, the University of Bristol (BA), the University of Durham (Cert. Counselling), King's College London (PhD) and the University of Sheffield (MEd), Percy started out in publishing (1984–88). He then trained for the priesthood at Durham and was ordained in 1991. In 1997 he became founding director of the Lincoln Theological Institute. He left in 2004 to become principal of Ripon College Cuddesdon, the principal UK Anglican training institution for ordination. During Percy's tenure it gained Observer status from Oxford. Percy argues for a "middle ground" between evangelical and catholic positions, taking (1) a progressive stance on LGBTQ rights and the ordination of women, but (2) an orthodox Christian position on the incarnation, atonement, resurrection, and ascension.

Academic and Bumps Standing The Norrington Table ranks Christ Church 6th on the 2006–16 average, 24th in 2016, 17th in 2017, and 11th in 2018. Christ Church has been

Head of the River 33 times during the life of Eights Week, most recently in 2017. In 2018 Summer Eights, Christ Church entered seven boats. The first men's boat was bumped twice, falling from 1st to 3rd place. The first women's boat was bumped once, falling from 3rd to 4th place. On points, Christ Church held its own in 2nd place behind Pembroke. On bumps, Christ Church had nothing to celebrate, suffering ten bumps.

CORPUS CHRISTI COLLEGE

Highlights

- Corpus Christi's arms shows the "vulning" pelican, a metaphor for the sacrifice of Jesus.
- Corpus was founded by Bishop Foxe of Winchester to train monks.
- Bishop Oldham of Exeter persuaded him to open it to humanists (non-monks).
- The college's pelican sundial is famed, as are the annual tortoise races.

Arms, Blazon *Tierced in Pale First Azure a Pelican in her piety Or vulned proper* (for Foxe) *Second Argent on an Escutcheon Gules two keys indorsed in bend the uppermost Argent the other Or a Sword interposed between them in bend sinister of the second pommel and hilt Gold* (for the See of Winchester) *ensigned of a Miter proper Third Sable a Chevron Or between three Owls Argent on a Chief of the second as many Roses Gules* (for Oldham).

Arms, Origin Ancient. Predates the College of Arms, founded in 1484.

Arms, Meaning The most prominent position of the *tierced in pale* (divided in three vertically), *dexter* (on the right from the perspective of the knight behind the shield), is allocated to the pelican, who was believed in the Middle Ages to pierce its own body (*vulning* or wounding itself) to obtain blood to feed its young. This is an allegory of Christ's self-sacrifice to save mankind. It is the shield of Bishop of Winchester Richard Foxe. The mitred arms of the See of Winchester are in the centre third, showing the keys of St Peter and the sword of St Paul. The sinister third of the shield is for Bishop of Exeter Hugh Oldham, whose canting arms give the owls (as in owldham), and whose birthplace in Lancashire inspires the red roses. Oldham gave the college its humanistic tradition.

Where Arms Can Be Seen Corpus Hall has a six-bay hammer-beam roof with a coat of arms of the founder, Bishop Foxe, at each end. The arms may be also seen on the boathouse.

Founded The College was founded in 1517, during the reign of young Henry VIII, by Richard Foxe, Bishop of Winchester. Bishop Oldham of Exeter gets credit for having persuaded Foxe to deviate from his original plan of making the college a monastic one, by opening it up to non-religious scholars. The original complement was twenty Fellows and twenty scholars. One of the founding fellows was Magdalen College alumnus Reginald Pole, the last Catholic Archbishop of Canterbury, under Mary I. Today the College has grown to 240 undergraduates and 115 graduate students, and 40 academic Fellows. It remains one of the smaller colleges.

*Corpus Christi College,
Main Quad with Pelican Sundial.*

Library and Archives The Library at Corpus Christi dates to the founding. The original first-floor Library (the old library) is still in use today, and contains bookcases dating from the late 16th/early 17th centuries. Corpus Library has two libraries, the modern main and the rare and archival library.

- The main library offers collections and services for students, with long opening hours and generous lending provisions. Access is restricted to authorised readers.

- The other, more specialized, library includes early printed books and manuscripts, largely assembled in the first 170 years after the College was founded. Bishop Foxe was a humanist. The trilingual library of Latin, Greek and Hebrew texts attracted praise from Erasmus, amongst others. This older collection is in protected space along with the College's Archives.The College has recently published two descriptive catalogues of its medieval manuscripts (Western and Greek); a third volume for the Hebrew manuscripts will follow.

16th century—The Sundial In the centre of the front quad was paid for by Corpus alumnus Charles Turnbull in 1581. In 1606 a perpetual calendar was painted on the side. When Thomas Arnold was a don at Corpus, before he became headmaster of Rugby School, he would sometimes throw bottles at this sundial. When queried why he did this, he explained: "It's the only thing I can throw bottles at, that won't throw them back at me."

21st century—The Tortoise Race Every year the college hosts a tortoise derby. Other colleges and tortoise keepers are invited to send competitors.

Current Head of House The current Acting President is Dr Helen Moore, Fellow and Tutor in English, until 30 September 2019. The 31st President, Sir Steven Charles Cow-ley, FRS, FREng, FInstP, was a theoretical physicist and international authority on nuclear fusion and astrophysical plasmas. He was the first President of Corpus Christi College to be a scientist. Cowley was educated at Corpus, and graduated with a BA in Physics in 1981. On 1 July 2018, he became director of the Princeton Plasma Physics Laboratory.

Academic and Bumps Standing On the Norrington Table, Corpus ranked 11th out of 30 colleges on the 2006–16 average, and a steady 15th in 2016, 2017, and 2018. The Corpus Men's Eight has been Head of the River twice, but not since 1885. In 2018 Summer Eights, the Corpus first men's eights had three bumps, rising from 28th to 25th place. The first women's eight held its own. On points, with 7 boats in the Isis, Corpus stayed at 29th place. On bumps, however, its 10 bumps put Corpus was in 3rd place.

EXETER COLLEGE

Highlights

- Exeter gets its name and its arms from the Bishop of Exeter.
- The inner-shield bends are for Walter Stapledon, the Bishop.
- The bends signify the River Exe, Devon; the keys are for the See of Exeter.
- Famed alumni include William Morris, J.R.R. Tolkien.

Arms, Blazon *Argent two Bendlets nebuly* (for Stapledon) *within a Bordure Sable charged with eight pairs of Gold Keys* (for the See of Exeter).

Arms, Origin Ancient. Predates the College of Arms, founded in 1484.

Arms, Meaning The eight pairs of keys, "addorsed and interlaced", are for St Peter. Each pair shows earth and heaven. The two guitar-head-like bends are called "bends nebully" and are the personal arms of Walter de Stapledon, who became Bishop of Exeter. The River Exe, the main river in Devon, is signified by the bends nebully.

Arms, Variations

- Argent two Bends nebulée with a Bordure Gules charged with eight pair of Keyes endorsed and interlaced in the rings Or the wards in chief. (The wards are the working ends of the keys, as in for-wards and back-wards.)
- Loggan's View of Exeter College (1675) shows 13 pairs of keys in the Bordure.
- Arms of Bishop Walter de Stapledon (1261–1326), Bishop of Exeter, detail from his monument in Exeter Cathedral (https://bit.ly/2JXxhI3). Shows Bars wavy and six pairs of keys in saltire.

14th century—Land holdings Founded in 1314 by the Devon-born Bishop of Exeter, the College has records showing its early history.

The Rector's accounts, kept by the head of the College, are on parchment rolls until the 16th century, along with the College estate records, i.e., deeds and other documents relating to land owned by the College.

16th century—Refounding The College was refounded by William Petre in 1566 and from this date institutional records include information on buildings, appointments and activities of Fellows and Rectors, and development of undergraduate teaching.

19th century—Societies From the mid-19th century a variety of sports clubs and societies started to flourish. The College records start including photographs of Exeter College students and alumni. The records are kept in purpose-built premises at Cohen Quad with controlled environmental storage and a reading room to accommodate researchers.

19th century—William Morris (1834–1896) studied Classics (Greats) at Oxford and became part of the Birmingham Set. He was an English textile designer, poet, novelist and activist socialist. A leader in the fashionable and successful British Arts and Crafts Movement, he was a major contributor to the revival of traditional British textile arts and methods of production. His novels helped establish the modern fantasy genre, while he played a significant role in strengthening Britain's first wave of socialism.

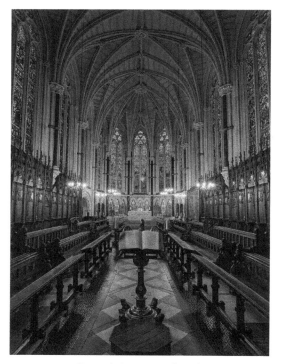

Exeter's imposing chapel.

20th century—J. R. R. Tolkien (1892–1973), while an undergraduate at Exeter, switched his examination school from Latin and Greek to English Language and Literature. So now he was required to study Old English! He became enamored of the *Crist* of Cynewulf, especially the couplet:

> *Eálá Earendel engla beorhtast*
> *Ofer middangeard monnum sended*

Which of course means:

Hail Earendel brightest of angels,
Over Middle Earth sent to men.

The idea for *Lord of the Rings* was surely born in Tolkien's head while a student at Exeter.

Current Head of House The Rector of Exeter College since 2014 (its 700th Anniversary year) is Sir Richard Hughes "Rick" Trainor KBE, FRHS, FAcSS. He was previously Principal of King's College London in 2004–14, where he oversaw the College's rise from 96th to 19th place in the QS World University Rankings (2015/16), making it the 5th-ranked UK university. He was previously Vice-Chancellor of the University of Greenwich in 2000–2004. Born in the United States, Trainor was educated at Calvert Hall College High School in Towson, Maryland. He graduated from Brown University with a BA summa cum laude in American Civilization. He subsequently earned MAs from Princeton University and from Merton College as a Rhodes Scholar, before completing his DPhil in 1981 at Nuffield College with a dissertation entitled "Authority and social structure in an industrialized area: A study of three Black Country towns, 1840–1890". Trainor is President of the Economic History Society. He was awarded an honorary knighthood (KBE) in June 2010 for services to UK higher education.

Academic and Bumps Standing The Norrington Table ranked Exeter in 21st place of 37 colleges and PPHs for the period 2006–2016. In 2016, Exeter ranked 27th of 36 colleges and PPHs. In 2017, Exeter was 29th of 35 colleges and PPHs. In 2018, Exeter ranked 18th of 30 colleges. Exeter and Christ Church were the third and fourth boats to enter the biennial intercollegiate racing, before there was an Oxford-Cambridge boat race. The boathouse coat of arms, shown on the boathouse that Exeter shares with Brasenose College, differs from the college's arms. More information on college boathouses, blades and blazers from The Oxbridge Pursuivant https://bit.ly/2BLyF0w. In 2018 Summer Eights, Exeter's first men's eight gained three bumps, rising from 26th place on the river to 23rd. The first women's eight fell from 23rd place to 24th place, with one net negative bump. With four boats entered, Exeter's overall point standing put it up from 26th to 24th place. With two net bumps, it ranked 15th.

GREEN TEMPLETON

Highlights

- Graduate school, for medicine and business.
- They merged in 2008 to focus on "human welfare".
- Green was a Brit who founded an American business.
- Templeton was an American who became a British investor.

Arms, Blazon *Or between two Flaunches Vert on each a Nautilus Shell the aperture outwards Or a Rod of Aesculapius Sable the Serpent Azure.*

Arms, Origin Original Grant, 4 Nov 2009. The arms were designed by Windsor Herald William Hunt, combining the arms of Green College and Templeton College in a remarkably elegant way.

Arms, Meaning The green tincture and the Rod of Asclepius are for Green College (founded by Dr Cecil Green). The Nautilus shell is from Templeton College (founded by Sir John Templeton), signifying the growth of companies and evolution of people.

Founded 2008 The college, the most recent new college at Oxford, was formed by merger of two existing colleges. (The number of colleges at Oxford in the 21st century has thereby fallen by one, from 39 to 38.) This graduate-only college has focused on human welfare, via a range of subjects including education, environment, health, management, medicine, and social policy. The College was created to rethink graduate education, built around an independent intellectual agenda and the management, medical and life sciences strengths of the two former colleges.

Merging Two Shields In September 2007, the College of Arms was given the task of designing a coat of arms for Oxford's newest college, utilizing the arms of Green and Templeton

Colleges. The task fell to Windsor Herald, then William D. Hunt. He designed a new coat of arms that incorporated (1) The Rod of Asclepius, symbol for the healing arts (Asclepius, the son of Apollo, was a practitioner of medicine in Greek mythology), the focal point of the Green College arms and (2) The nautilus shell, which symbolises evolution and renewal, chosen by Sir John Templeton and adopted by Templeton College in 1984.

The Full Achievement In Windsor Herald's full achievement of the Green Templeton arms, the crest represents the sun behind the astronomical symbol for Venus (♀), homage to the transit of Venus across the sun in 1761. This event famously drew attention to the lack of locations in Britain to observe the transit and led to the building of the Radcliffe Observatory. Green College was blessed with the 18th century buildings of the Observatory's buildings and surroundings in North Oxford, and this site has been retained by Green Templeton.

Green—Dr Cecil Howard Green, KBE was born in Whitefield, England on August 6, 1900, moved to British Columbia to study and finished his doctorate in electrical engineering at M.I.T. He founded Texas Instruments. He made a major gift to Oxford to create Green College in 1979 as a place to bring together increasing numbers of graduate students in medicine and related disciplines and especially to encourage enterprises whereby industry made use of academic knowledge. Dr Green died April 11, 2003 at 102 years old.

Templeton—Sir John Marks Templeton While Dr Green went west from England to Canada and the USA, John Templeton went east, originally on a Rhodes Scholarship. He was born November 12, 1912 in Winchester, Tennessee. When he got straight As on his first first-grade report card, his father made a deal, as Templeton told CNN: "Well now, each time you get anything less than an A, you give me a bale of cotton, and each time you get nothing except As, I will give you a bale of cotton." Templeton commented that his father thought that his son would wind up owing his father a lot of bales of cotton, and upon graduation the debt would be forgiven. But twelve years later, when Templeton graduated from high school first in his class, his father owed him 22 bales, and the son forgave his father's debt. He was the first in his town to attend college. He went to Yale, where young Templeton helped pay his college bill with poker winnings from his contemporaries. Templeton went on to Oxford and stayed in England, becoming a British citizen, investor, and fund manager. In 1954, he created the Templeton Growth Fund, an early mutual fund, where he became known as "arguably the best stock-picker in the 20th century" (*Money Magazine*). His interest was in growth—of corporations and people (through their spiritual evolution). In 1984, Templeton College succeeded the Oxford Centre for Management Studies, founded in 1959 by Clifford Barclay to provide continuing management education. Templeton College was granted a Royal Charter in 1995 and was based at Egrove Park in the village of Kennington, outside of Oxford. The Kennington buildings are now occupied by Oxford's Saïd Business School. John Templeton died July 8, 2008, in Nassau, Bahamas.

Current Head of House The Principal since 2015 has been Denise Anne Lievesley, CBE, FAcSS, who was previously Chief Executive

of the English Information Centre for Health and Social Care, Director of Statistics at UNESCO, and Director (1991–1997) of what is now the UK Data Archive. Lievesley served as Professor of Research Methods at the University of Essex. She has also served as a United Nations Special Adviser on Statistics, President of the Royal Statistical Society (1999–2001), President of the International Statistical Institute (2007–2009), and the International Association for Official Statistics. In 2014 she was appointed Commander of the Order of the British Empire (CBE), for services to social science.

Green Templeton tie on display for sale.

Academic and Bumps Standing As a graduate college, Green Templeton is not in the Norrington Table. But it competed on the river in Eights Week 2018, with four crews, one men's and three women's. The men's crew began in 44th place (out of 92 boats) and made two bumps. The first women's crew bumped every one of the four days. The second boat bumped once. The third boat held its own. Overall, Green Templeton (GTC) advanced from 32nd to 31st place.

HARRIS MANCHESTER COLLEGE

Highlights

- Warrington Academy was earlier incarnation.
- Manchester Academy founded 1786 as a Unitarian Center.
- Moved to Oxford in 1889 after University admitted Dissenters.
- Became an Oxford College for "mature students" in 1996.

Arms, Blazon *Torches inflamed in saltire proper on a Chief Argent between two Roses of the field barbed and seeded an open Book also proper.*

Arms, Origin Original Grant 14 May 1934.

Arms, Meaning The red roses in chief represent Lancashire, of which Manchester is one of the two largest cities and where the college's prior incarnation of Manchester Academy was located. The two torches in base represent enlightenment and the open, blank book represents access to learning but with no commitment to divine revelation. The torches are interpreted artistically with wide latitude.

Arms, Where Visible The arms are on the front gate.

Founded 1786 as Manchester Academy, ". . . for those of all faiths and none", succeeding the Warrington Academy, which had previously succeeded Richard Frankland's Rathmell Academy in Yorkshire. Moved from Manchester to Oxford in 1889, after dissenters were admitted, and became a full Oxford College in 1996. Harris Manchester is the only college at Oxford restricting its student body to "mature" students—at least 21 years old.

17th century—Rathmell Academy Richard Frankland's Rathmell Academy was founded in Yorkshire in 1670. The Warrington Academy, called "the cradle of Unitarianism," succeeded it.

18th century Warrington and Manchester Academies English Presbyterians helped found, through legacies, the Warrington Academy (1757–1786). In 1761, Joseph Priestley moved to Warrington to be tutor of modern languages and rhetoric, having just published a new English grammar. By the 1780s, the influences at Warrington Academy were strongly Unitarian. Its successor Manchester Academy was founded in Manchester in 1786 by Unitarians. Portraits of two of the founders—Thomas Barnes and Thomas Percival—may be seen in the College's Warrington Window. The third founder was Ralph Harrison, to whom a beautiful window (William Morris from a design by Burne-Jones) is dedicated in the College Chapel. All three founders were graduates of the Warrington Academy and two, Barnes and Harrison, were ministers at Manchester's Unitarian Cross Street Chapel. Harris Manchester College is the direct and unbroken descendant of the Manchester Academy.

19th century—Royal Patronage A young Queen Victoria signed a Royal Warrant giving the Manchester Academy the status of a college of London University, almost 50 years before it moved to Oxford. (The right of dissenters to attend Oxford was taken away by Queen Elizabeth I and was restored by Queen Victoria.) The first Oxford premises were at 90 High Street. Manchester College then moved to Mansfield Road in 1893.

Harris Manchester College arms on gate.

20th century—College Status For a hundred years, Manchester College was, like Regent's Park College today, not a full college although it had the name (Regent's Park College is a Permanent Private Hall).

In 1996 a £3.6 million gift from Lord Harris of Peckham (knighted 1985; made life peer 1996) enabled Manchester College to become a full Oxford college. With his donation the college was renamed Harris Manchester and a statue in army uniform of Lord Harris's father (who died suddenly when his son was just 15) was permanently located in a garden outside the lodgings of the Head of House. Opponents of the change included members of the Unitarian church, since to become a college the size of the student body would have to grow and control by a religious denomination or movement would have to diminish, although exceptions have been made for colleges affiliated with the Church of England.

20th century—Lord Harris Following in his father's footsteps, Lord Harris was chairman and chief executive of Harris Carpets, which incorporated Queensway in 1977. The expanded company was acquired in 1988 and Lord Harris then became Chairman of Carpetright plc, now his son Martin's company, until 2014. For 18 years until July 2004, Lord Harris was also a non-executive director of Great Universal Stores plc. He was an admirer of Mrs Thatcher and contributor also to David Cameron. However, he protested Conservative policies when he felt they were cutting too deeply into funding for schools. More than 40 of the new Academies bear his name, and he has been said to have done "more to help working-class children than any Labour politician since Attlee and Bevan". Educated at Streatham Grammar School in Lambeth, London, Philip Harris in 1960 married Pauline Chumley (DBE, 2004) and they have three other children besides Martin. Lord Harris turned 76 on September 15, 2018.

Current Head of House The Principal since 1988 is Sir Ralph Waller KBE, the longest-serving head of house in Oxford's history. He is also a Pro-Vice Chancellor of the University. Rev Waller is an ordained Methodist minister and Director of the Farmington Institute for Christian Studies. Born in Lincolnshire, Waller was educated at the University of London (BD) and the University of Nottingham (MTh) and completed a PhD at King's College London with a thesis on James Martineau, an influential Unitarian minister and philosopher.

Academic and Bumps Standing On the Norrington Table, Harris Manchester ranked 30th for the average of 2000–2016, 11th in 2016, 27th in 2017, and 30th in 2018. It does not compete in Torpids or Summer Eights, but has an affiliation with Wadham College that allows eligible Harris Manchester students to row in Wadham eights.

HERTFORD COLLEGE

Highlights

- Founded by Elias de Hertford as Hart Hall.
- The "canting" arms feature a hart (medieval word for a stag).
- Refounded by Dr Richard Newton, and again by Thomas Baring.
- Accepted the first black U.S. Rhodes Scholar in 1907.

Arms, Blazon *Gules a Hart's Head caboshed Argent between the Attires a Cross patty fitched in the foot Or.*

Arms, Origin Hertford deliberately chose not to obtain a grant of arms because Henry VIII exempted Oxford and Cambridge colleges from the requirement that institutions obtain a grant from, and submit to visits by, heralds from the College of Arms. Sidney Graves Hamilton suggests this in his 1903 book on Hertford College. In 1574, herald Richard Lee, Portcullis Pursuivant, visited Oxford and no objections were recorded. But 60 years later, in 1634, the University did object, citing the exemption it was given by Henry VIII. Hertford was therefore not included in the post-Restoration (Charles II and later) visitations. Since Oxford University claimed exemption from deference to the College of Arms, Hamilton argues that it would have been viewed as an "act of treachery" for a college to accede to the visit!

Arms, Meaning The *canting* (punning) shield shows a "hart" to convey the name of the first "founder". The motto references the "ford"—i.e., the *fontes aquarum,* or "fountains of water". The patty cross is narrower at the center, giving it the look of four paws (pattés). The fitch at the bottom is a stake to drive the cross into the ground. The cross references the fact that Hart Hall was a haven for recusant Catholics.

13th century—Elias de Hertford The original Hart Hall was founded in 1283, but did not operate like a modern college. The man who

gave his name to Hertford College purchased the hall in 1283. John de Dokelynton bought it from Elias de Hertford Jr., having also acquired another tenement (Arthur Hall) in the parish, and in 1312 he sold the two properties to Walter de Stapeldon, Bishop of Exeter. Stapeldon intended to found a college for poor students in Oxford, and in 1314 he installed twelve scholars in Hart Hall, but a year later he removed his scholars to what is now Exeter College. Exeter then leased out Hart and Arthur Halls to MAs as academic halls. One distinguished tenant was William of Wykeham, who used the halls for his scholars while New College was being built for them. The string of New College Fellows who served as Warden of the halls includes Richard Tonworth, Nicholas Wykeham, Thomas Cranleigh (afterwards Archbishop of Dublin), John Walter, William Ware, and John Wytham. By the time New College was finished, the halls had been leased for 21 years, twice the length of the usual lease.

16th century—St Alexander Briant Alexander Briant came up to Hart Hall in the 1570s, when the Hall was known as a refuge in the Elizabethan era for recusant Catholics, who continued in their religion rather than seek compromise with the established Church of England. Alexander was influenced by Richard Holtby, his tutor at Hart Hall, to seek a religious life as a Jesuit. Ordained in France, Fr Alexander returned to his home county of Somerset to minister to Catholics, an activity that was treasonous under the English laws of the time. At 25, he was arrested and tortured, and was executed for treason at Tyburn on 1 December 1581, along with fellow Jesuit Fr Edmund Campion, after whom Campion Hall is named. Alexander joined Edmund as a Catholic saint in 1970.

Hertford College Quad.

18th century—Dr Newton The true founder of Hertford College was Dr Richard Newton, who became Principal in 1710 and gave the first endowment to his college. He attempted to give it statutes and incorporated it as "The Principal and Fellows of Hertford College" but it was only partially converted to what we would today consider a college, especially since the Principal retained financial control as Bursar. Dr Newton's plan favored "disputations" as an educational tool and required undergraduates to dispute in philosophy and his graduates to dispute in theology. Newton wanted 32 undergraduates, eight to come up each year in the charge of a tutor, with whom they were to live in one angle of the quadrangle. The eight would be served by a bedmaker, and one "servitor", a paid student. The tutors were to be MAs. In 1720 he published Statutes for Hart Hall. Newton lectured Thursdays to all the undergraduates, and the tutors lectured to their pupils on the other weekdays. Three times a week tutors had to give a lecture, which consisted of reading from and commenting upon a set book. Every undergraduate had to write a weekly essay and read it out to the whole college on Saturday. The college was intended to educate clergymen, but welcomed "gentlemen commoners" from moderately well-off families. The commoners had the same rooms, food, teaching, and discipline as the others but paid double fees. Dr Newton's egalitarianism was greatly opposed in Oxford. When Dr Newton presented his petition for a royal charter in 1723, his landlords, Exeter College, immediately opposed it. But the Attorney General in 1724 found in favour of the Principal of Hart Hall and within six years he had completed at his own expense one-quarter of his rebuilding plan. He also built a chapel. His Statutes for Hart Hall became, in 1747, the "Statutes of Hertford College".

19th century—Thomas Baring Alas, over the next century Hertford College was mismanaged and went out of business. In 1874 Magdalen Hall took over the name as it sought college status, having been given additional support from Thomas Baring.

20th century—Alain LeRoy Locke. The first African-American Rhodes Scholar, Alain Locke, was elected in 1907. When he arrived at Oxford, he was rejected by several colleges to which he applied, based on his race. Some Rhodes Scholars from southern states would not associate with him. Hertford eventually took him in. It would be 1960 before the next African-American was selected for a Rhodes Scholarship.

Current Head of House The Principal of Hertford since 2011 is William Nicolas Hutton, who is also Chair of the Big Innovation Centre, an initiative of the Work Foundation, of which Hutton was chief executive in 2002–2008. He is known for his advocacy of centre-left policies. Hutton began his education in Scotland, finishing at Chislehurst and Sidcup Grammar School. After studying sociology and economics at the University of Bristol, gaining a BSocSc, he started as an equity salesman for a stock broker, before leaving to study for an MBA at INSEAD. Hutton moved on to work for ten years with the BBC, for a time as economics correspondent for *Newsnight,* in 1983–88. He spent four years as editor-in-chief at *The Observer* before joining The Work Foundation. He has written *The State We're In,* on Britain in the 1990s from a social democratic point of view and *The World We're In*, on the U.S.European relationship, emphasising differences between the two blocs, with the UK between them. Hutton's book *The Writing on the Wall* examines the rise of China and its increasingly unsustainable contradictions. He supports the European Union and rejects American conservatism.

Academic and Rowing Standing The Norrington Table ranks Hertford as 13th for the 2006–16 period, 20th in 2016, 24th in 2017, and 27th in 2018. Hertford was Head of the River once, in 1881. In Eights Week 2018, Hertford filled four boats, two men's and two women's. The first men's boat started at 16th and held its place. The first women's boat started at 9th and was bumped three times. Overall, Hertford dropped from 12th place to 15th on points.

JESUS COLLEGE

Highlights

- Large contingent of Welsh students and dons.
- Oxford's only college established under Elizabeth I.
- Arms are those of Rotherham, a Yorkshire man, not clear why.
- Famed alumni include T. E. Lawrence, "Lawrence of Arabia".

Arms, Blazon *Vert three Stags trippant Argent attired Or* (for Price).

Arms, Origin "It's not easy being green (*vert*)." For one thing, the tincture is the least popular among the colleges of the four main ones, one-fourth as popular as red (*gules*) and half as popular as blue (*azure*) and black (*sable,* like French sand). The Jesus College arms are blazoned to show a green (*vert*) field, three silver (*argent*) stags, one foreleg up (*trippant*), with golden (*or*) antlers and hooves. It was once thought that the the green (*vert*) field was an error, because the earliest depiction of the Jesus arms was about 1590, in a document held by the College of Arms, and this refers to the stags as having a blue (*azure*) field. However, Peter O'Donoghue, then Bluemantle Pursuivant (since 2012 York Herald), reported the blue (*azure*) field appeared 90 years later, on John Speed's 1605 Map of Oxfordshire. So green (*vert*) may have been the original color. A version of the arms with a green (*vert*) field

dates back to 1619, in an armorial quarry painted by one of the Van Linge brothers. Green was generally used by 1730, although horizontal hatchings (indicating *azure*) were still used on college bookplates as late as 1761.

Arms, Meaning The shield is that of Thomas Rotherham, Bishop of Lincoln. At the time of foundation, the See of Lincoln included Oxford. Rotherham later became Archbishop of York. He was born in Yorkshire and was educated as a young boy by a much-appreciated teacher of grammar, after which he was sent to the newly founded Eton College to prepare for university entrance. Rotherham was educated at King's College, Cambridge, where he became a Fellow. He became Bishop of Rochester in 1468, Bishop of Lincoln in 1472, and Archbishop of York in 1480, a position he held until 1500. In 1467, King Edward IV appointed Rotherham Keeper of the Privy Seal. In 1475 he became Lord Chancellor. Between 1477 and his death,

Rotherham was the owner of Barnes Hall in South Yorkshire. All of which explains why Rotherham was important . . . but not why his arms are on the Jesus shield. He doesn't seem to have done anything for Jesus College other than landlord-related activities compensated by rent payments, whereas he did endow neighboring Lincoln College.

Arms, Nominee The College is named for Jesus Christ. The name is a historic one from the date of foundation, at the instigation of the Treasurer of St David's Cathedral in Wales. The college has always had a special appeal to applicants from Wales. Between 1571 and 1915, only one Principal was not from Wales or of Welsh descent. Jesus is often referred to as "the Welsh college" and is where the university's Professor of Celtic resides.

How Active the Stags? With new research showing that even moderate activity extends one's life, the difference between the Jesus arms and the Lincoln arms takes on new meaning. The Lincoln arms shows the three stags *statant*, i.e., standing still with all four hooves on the ground. The Jesus arms show the stags *trippant*, with a foreleg in the air. Apart from providing a better guide to a longevity-extending, active lifestyle, the *trippant* position is the one assumed in the arms of the founder, Bishop Thomas Rotherham in an authenticated portrait in Lincoln's Hall.

Founded Jesus was founded in 1571, during the reign of Elizabeth I. It was the only Oxford college founded during her 44-year reign.

15th century—What's Rotherham's Connection with Jesus? Jesus College is on Turl Street (we called it "the Turl"), of which the joke is often told: "Q. How is the Church of England like Turl Street?" "A. It runs from the High to the Broad and it has Jesus." But the relationship between Rotherham and Jesus College seems actually to have just been financial. Rotherham was the landlord of a property that became part of Jesus College. Lincoln College loyalists have claimed that Jesus stole their three stags from their neighbor. A more likely story is that both colleges derived their arms from the same man, Bishop Rotherham, who had three stags in his arms. Paul Langford, former Lincoln Rector, has suggested that Jesus College adopted the arms of a theological college founded by Rotherham in his home town—Jesus College, Rotherham—which had been suppressed in the time of Edward VI, but why Jesus would do that is unclear. For whatever reason, the arms of the College are surely those of Bishop Rotherham, and the best explanation is that John Speed saw them on Lawrence Hall in Ship Street, a building given to Rotherham in 1476.It was leased to Jesus College starting 1572; Speed drew his map of Oxford in 1605. The Rotherham-Jesus arms were already very different from those of Lincoln, because as of 1574 Lincoln's tierced shield was confirmed by Richard Lee, Portcullis Pursuivant, with stags *statant* and *or*.

20th century—Lawrence of Arabia T.E. Lawrence was a legendary British soldier and famed Jesus alumnus. Born in Termed, Wales, he naturally gravitated to Oxford's Welsh College. He studied Arabic, joined the British army as an intelligence officer in 1914 and spent a year in Cairo, Egypt. He was then recruited to help address problems created by the Emir of Mecca's revolt against Turkish rule. In 1916, he accompanied a British diplomat to Arabia, where he was sent to join the army of the Emir's son as a liaison officer. Under Lawrence's guidance, the Arabians launched an effective guerrilla war and he was lionized by the Bedouins. In July 1917, Arabian forces captured Aqaba and joined the British march on Jerusalem. Lawrence was promoted to lieutenant colonel. In November that year, he was captured behind Turkish lines in Arab dress and was tortured and sexually abused before escaping. He rejoined his army, which was advancing on Damascus. When Damascus fell on October 1, 1918, Arabia was liberated, but Lawrence despaired over Arabian factionalism.

Disillusioned, he left for England, heart-broken that Britain had encouraged inter-Arab hostilities. When he appeared before King George V, he declined the medals offered to him. After the war, he lobbied hard for independence for Arab countries and wrote a war memoir, *The Seven Pillars of Wisdom.* He enlisted in the Royal Air Force (RAF) under an assumed name, was discharged from the RAF in 1935, and just a few months later was fatally injured in a motorcycle accident.

Current Head of House The Principal since 2015 is Professor Sir Nigel Shadbolt, Professorial Research Fellow in the Department of Computer Science, University of Oxford. He is Chairman of the Open Data Institute, which he co-founded in 2012 with Tim Berners-Lee. Born in London, he grew up in the Derbyshire village of Ashford-in-the-Water. He earned an undergraduate degree at Newcastle University. His PhD is from the Department of Artificial Intelligence at the University of Edinburgh. Shadbolt coauthored a book on privacy and trust in the Digital Age, *The Spy in the Coffee Machine.* In 2007–11 Shadbolt was Deputy Head of the School of Electronics and Computer Science (ECS) at the University of Southampton and in 2011–2014 he was Head of its Web and Internet Science Group, the first research group dedicated to the study of Web science and Internet science, within ECS. The Semantic Web research led to the formation of Garlik, offering identity protection services, and in 2008, Garlik won the UK BT Flagship IT Award. Experian acquired

Garlik in 2011. In 2009 he and Tim Berners-Lee were appointed Information Advisors to the UK Government. The two led a team to develop data.gov.uk, a single point of access for UK non-personal public data.

Jesus College boathouse.

Academic and Bumps Standing The Norrington Table ranked Jesus 12th on the 2006–16 average, 14th in 2016, 18th in 2017, jumping to 6th in 2018. The best shot that Jesus had of being Head of the River was in 1815 and 1816, when the only opponent was Brasenose. Unfortunately BNC won both years and Jesus never prevailed in the many races since, with added competitors. In Eights Week, Jesus filled seven boats, four men's and three women's. The first men's boat started at 15th and bumped three of the four days, the first women's boat started at 19th and bumped each one of the four days. Overall, Jesus rose from 13th to 12th place.

KEBLE COLLEGE

Highlights

- The College arms are those of John Keble, Tractarian.
- The Keble arms date back at least to the 16th century.
- Keble, Pusey, and Newman were at the heart of the "Oxford Movement"
- Keble College's Holy Zebra brickwork is unique in Oxford.

Arms, Blazon *Argent a Chevron engrailed Gules on a Chief Azure three Mullets pierced Or* (for Keble).

Arms, Origin The arms are from the Keybell/Keble family. An identical coat of arms was confirmed in 1510 to an ancestor, Henry Keybell, who was Lord Mayor of London that year.

Arms, Nominee The arms are those of Rev. John Keble (1792–1866), in whose memory the College was founded and named. Keble sparked the Tractarian movement, also known as the Oxford Movement, with a sermon in 1833 that complained of "national apostacy". The Tractarians sought to recover the medieval Roman Catholic writings and spiritual heritage for the Church of England. Funding for the new College was sought from Tractarian sympathisers, including Chapel benefactor William Gibbs, whose family's fortune was based on Peruvian bird droppings (guano) sold as fertiliser.

Founded In 1870, Keble College opened with thirty students. The Chapel was opened in 1876.

19th century—John Keble and Tractarianism

Three people closely associated with Tractarianism were John Keble, Edward Bouverie Pusey and John Henry Newman. While generally considered as "High Church" reform in contrast to the overlapping contemporary reforms of the "Low Church" Evangelicals within the Church of England, the Tractarian rediscovery of medieval Catholicism had its own kind of

excitement, deepening public understanding of Christianity and energizing their faith. Keble and Pusey remained in the Anglican Church, while Newman converted to Catholicism and was followed by some other leading Anglicans. The Pope made Newman a Cardinal but insisted that Newman not return to Oxford. His conversion made Tractarianism suspect among Anglicans and it never recovered from Newman's defection. The split was echoed in the next century with the rift between Oxford dons and close friends J. R. R. Tolkien and C. S. Lewis.

Keble College.

19th century—Holy Zebra Architecture

Architect William Butterfield did things with brickwork that were described as a "Holy Zebra" style, meant perhaps to imitate the Cathedral in Siena, Italy and assert a High Church affiliation. A French visitor is said to have asked, looking up at the college, *C'est magnifique, mais ce n'est pas la gare?* ("It is magnificent, but this is not the railway station?")

The splendid Keble Chapel is widely praised.

19th century—Keble College's Beginnings

The college that Keble founded went in directions that he might not have. Its first Warden, Edward Talbot, took up the cause of a place for women at Oxford's colleges and is recognized for this in the Talbot dogs in the arms of Lady Margaret Hall. (Keble College itself did not admit women undergraduates until 1979.) Talbot encouraged the teaching of science and endorsed the scientific merit of the theory of evolution, while maintaining Anglican orthodoxy. Keble College students also early on engaged in unofficial boxing matches where alcohol flowed.

Current Head of House Keble elected its first female Warden in 1994. The Warden since 2010 is Sir Jonathan Phillips, KCB, former Permanent Secretary of the Northern Ireland Office in 2005–2010.

Academic and Bumps Standing Keble ranked 18th in the Norrington Table for 2006–2016, moved up to 17th in 2016, 12th in 2017, and fell back to 23rd in 2018. On the river, Keble is a powerhouse, as the men's first eight bumped Christ Church in the 2018 Summer Eights to become Head of the River. The first women's eight started in 5th place and fell to 6th (out of 78 women's boats). Keble filled three men's boats and two women's. The overall Keble ranking fell from 3rd to 4th.

KELLOGG COLLEGE

Highlights

- The arms were freshly designed to show the college mission and patron.
- Kellogg was founded to serve people pursuing continuing education programs.
- Uniquely, Kellogg's arms honour a corporate benefactor with a key product ingredient.
- Oxford Chancellor Lord Patten describes the College as a "jewel".

Arms, Blazon *Per pale indented Argent and Azure on the Argent a Chevron enhanced Gules in base a Book Azure leaved Argent on the Azure an ear of Wheat palewise Or the whole within a bordure Gules.*

Arms, Origin Arms granted 1999.

Arms, Nominee The U.S. cereal manufacturer maker W[ill] K[eith] Kellogg, who started his company in 1906 in Battle Creek, Michigan and his foundation in 1930. The Kellogg Foundation was a principal funder of the creation of the College.

Arms, Meaning Kellogg Foundation support of the College's foundation is symbolized by the ear (also called a spike or head, each with 20–30 grains or kernels) of wheat (*sinister* side), which is an attributed symbol of the Kellogg Foundation, created by the founder from income from Kellogg's Corn Flakes and other breakfast foods made from grains. Its coat of arms is a brand within a brand. The book (*dexter*) represents learning without the link to the Bible and piety evoked by Latin words as in older arms, under a chevron suggesting shelter.

Arms, Use The Kellogg College coat of arms is well utilized, appearing on signs and decorations and items prominently displayed for sale—more than any other college that the author has visited.

19th century Kellogg's origins are in the movement to open Oxford up to more students (see History of Oxford above, 19th century after 1845). The Oxford Extension movement had both social and political aims, educating the larger community to achieve a better informed democracy. Kellogg College celebrated its 25th anniversary in 2015. As with other graduate colleges at Oxford like Nuffield, Kellogg College has an egalitarian ethos, as shown by a lack of a high table in the dining room. Uniquely among Oxbridge colleges, its grace is in Welsh, chosen to commemorate the foundation of the College in 1990.

20th century, Founded 1990 The college came into being on St David's Day, 1 March 1990, as Rewley House. It was renamed in honour of W. K. Kellogg in 1994, in recognition of support by the W. K. Kellogg Foundation over the preceding decades.The college has close connections with the university's departments for continuing education, medicine, education, computer science, and law, and other departments active in areas of professional and part-time study.

21st century Kellogg College is the first home for part-time students at Oxford. Many of its students continue to work in their professions while they study. As of the 2018 academic year, the student body numbers 1139 students, of whom 268 are attending full-time and 871 part-time. The college has been coeducational since its foundation. In 2004, the college acquired a site for a new home between Banbury Road and Bradmore Road, in the Norham Manor area of North Oxford. The College offices moved there in 2006. In 2017, the Hub was opened, with Kellogg College's Common Room and café.

Patten Calls Kellogg a "Jewel" Oxford Chancellor Lord Patten of Barnes, in March 2015, at the 25th Anniversary of the College's foundation, described Kellogg as one of the "jewels in the crown" of the University. Lord Patten supports the college's creating greater access to higher education for those unable to be full-time residential students, such as the elderly or people living a long distance away. Kellogg has the most international students, from the largest number of countries, of any Oxford college. They study a wide range of subjects, from International Human Rights Law, to Sustainable Urban Development, to Evidence-Based Health Care. Kellogg and St Cross are the only colleges without a royal charter. Officially "societies" of the university, for accounting purposes St Cross and Kellogg are considered departments of the university.

Current Head of House The President since 2007 is Jonathan Michie, who studied at Balliol for his BA. He earned an MSc in Economics from Queen Mary University of London and a DPhil in economics from Oxford. He also serves director of the Oxford University Department for Continuing Education, and serves as President of Kellogg College *ex officio*. After seven years teaching at Cambridge, Michie became Head of the School of Management & Organizational Psychology at Birbeck College, University of London. In 2004, he became Director of the Birmingham Business School.

*Kellogg College blades,
rowing with Christ Church.*

Academic and Bumps Standing Since Kellogg College serves continuing education students, and they do not sit for undergraduate examinations, as Kellogg is not included in the Norrington Table. It also does not compete as a college in intercollegiate rowing. It does contribute players to University teams—the Oxford rugby squads that beat Cambridge in the 2011 and 2012 included seven or more Kellogg students. Kellogg students also rowed against Cambridge in 2013 in the University's victorious men's, women's, women's lightweight and reserve boats.

LADY MARGARET HALL

Highlights

- Suggested by the first Warden of Keble College, Edward Talbot.
- For his bravery, he is given two talbot dogs in the LMH shield.
- The portcullis is for Lady Margaret, the bell for Wordsworth.
- LMH was the first women's college, for Anglican women students.

Arms, Blazon *Or on a Chevron between in chief two Talbots passant and in base a Bell Azure a Portcullis of the field.*

Arms, Origin Assumed. The arms were adopted without the formality of applying to the College of Arms.

Arms, Meaning The talbots in chief appear as supporters of the arms of Dr Edward Talbot, the first Warden of Keble and later Bishop, who promoted the idea of a woman's college that became LMH. The port-cullis is from the arms of Lady Margaret Beaufort. The bell is from the Wordsworth coat of arms, a remembrance of the family of the first Principal. Lady Margaret is reemphasized in the full achievement by the adoption of her Beaufort family Motto: SOUVENT ME SOUVIENS ("I often remember.")

Arms, Nominees The college is named after Lady Margaret Beaufort, Countess of Richmond and mother of Henry VII. On 21 November 1878, Elizabeth Wordsworth, daughter of the Bishop of Lincoln, became the first Principal of the Hall. At her suggestion it was named after Lady Margaret, whom she called: "A scholar, a gentlewoman and a saint".

Founded In 1878, Dr. Talbot proposed the creation of Lady Margaret Hall, and in 1879 the Bishop of Oxford opened it with nine students in residence. LMH was constituted under a Deed of Trust in 1892 and its property vested in three trustees, making LMH largely independent. In 1913 LMH became a not-for-profit Limited Liability Company, under the Companies Act (1908), and in 1926 was incorporated by Royal Charter under the name of "The Principal, Council, and Members of Lady Margaret Hall". This charter uniquely incorporates not only the Principal and council, but also students ("Members")—past, present, and future. By a decree of Convocation 15 June 1920, LMH was admitted to the privileges, whatever they are, conferred by Stat. Tit. XXIII of Women Students. The government of LMH is vested in a council consisting of 24 members, which includes the Principal, treasurer, official and professorial fellows, and not less than six elected members called councillors. One outcome of coeducation in the men's colleges (and, as of 2017, all six Permanent Private Halls) is that all the women's colleges at Oxford also now admit men.

19th century—Oxford Makes a Bet on Women When Dr Talbot proposed in 1878 to a committee of interested persons a hall for women students, he earned permanent memorialization in the LMH coat of arms. However, his concept was experimental, to "attempt" the establishment of "a small hall" that would be connected "with the Church of England". The University had drawn up a curriculum for women in Oxford. To avoid disrupting the men, women were parked in their own residence hall. At first only one hall was envisioned, operating on Church of England principles. But dissenters had been gaining places at Oxford and they argued for a dissenters' residence hall, which became Somerville College. To supervise these risky trials, an Association for the Education of Women was created and it remained vigilant for 15 years before LMH and Somerville were patched into the tight weave of the University.

LMH students picnic on the Cherwell, 100 years ago.

19th century—Opposition from Elizabeth Sewell It may be hard for some to imagine the opposition that Talbot's plan generated in 1878, from both men and women. Elizabeth Sewell, a prominent writer and educator of young girls, and sister of the Warden of New College, said: "I think the competition with young men highly undesirable, and the unavoidable publicity in a place of comparatively small size dangerous to women at an age so open to vanity and excitement."

20th century—First Woman Speaks at the Oxford Union Lucy Sutherland (then at Somerville) was the first woman undergraduate to speak at the Oxford Union, winning applause in 1926 for her opposition to the motion "That the women's colleges . . . should be leveled to the ground". Sutherland went on to become LMH's fourth Principal, 1945–71, succeeding Dame Elizabeth Wordsworth, 1878–1909; Henrietta Jex-Blake, 1909–1921; and Lynda Grier, 1921–1945.

20th century—Shock! American Benefactor Didn't Want Credit LMH took a major step forward when Mrs. Edward S. Harkness of New York in 1930 added £35,000 to earlier benefactions to expand the college. She had been inspired by Margaret Deneke, who went on a musical tour of the United States to raise money for the hall. Mrs. Harkness made a special request that the Hall name the new wing after "those who worked for it and not after those who merely gave money". So, in a radical break with tradition, it was named after Deneke.

Current Head of House The Principal since 2015 is Alan Rusbridger, who attended Magdalene College, Cambridge. He was formerly editor-in-chief of *The Guardian* (his successor at *The Guardian*, Katharine Viner, attended Pembroke College, Oxford). In 2014 he was awarded in Stockholm the "Alternative Nobel Prize", the Right Livelihood Award. He has pioneered the widely admired LMH Foundation Year program (https://bit.ly/2PVT7xN), now recruiting for its fourth year.

Academic and Bumps Standing The Norrington Table shows a rising rank for LMH. The College was 28th based on the average for 2006–16, rose to 23rd in 2016, to 16th in 2017. It fell back to 21st place in 2018. It had five boats entered in the 2018 Eights Week. The first men's boat entered at 14th and was bumped once. The first women's boat entered at 24th and bumped twice. The overall standing of LMH rose from 19th to 18th place.

LINACRE COLLEGE

Highlights

- The Linacre arms reference the Bible and the St James Pilgrimage (Camino de Santiago).
- Linacre was a physician and an outstanding scholar.
- Linacre received a royal charter and became a full Oxford college in 1986.
- Arms were designed afresh and granted in 1988.

Arms, Blazon *Sable an open Book proper edged Or bound Gules the dexter page charged with the Greek Letter Alpha the sinister page charged with the Greek Letter Omega both Sable the whole between three Escallops Argent.*

Arms, Origin Original Grant 8 December 1988.

Arms, Meaning The arms reference Thomas Linacre, the founder. The book implies learning, and the Greek letters suggest that the book is the Bible (the Book of Revelation references Christ as the alpha and omega). The scallop shell traditionally references St James and in particular the *Camino de Santiago* (the Way of St James). A shell is typically worn by pilgrims, and scallops on a coat of arms often imply that the bearer or ancestor did the pilgrimage to Santiago de Compostela.

Arms, Nominee The Founder, Dr Thomas Linacre, created the Royal College of Physicians. He left his fortune to endow professorships in Greek medicine at Oxford and Cambridge. Linacre admits only graduate students. It was the first coeducational college at Oxford.

16th century—Did Dr Linacre Become a "Catholic" Priest?

A historian of Catholic scientists concludes that the men in his book are "Catholic clergymen of high standing, and none of them suffered anything like persecution for his opinions." Linacre's call to the priesthood from medicine is sometimes described as a rejection of the papal hierarchy in favor of simple parochial service. Dr Linacre was the best known physician of his time in England, the greatest scholar of the English Renaissance period, and founder of the Royal College of Physicians. He had all his life been on intimate terms with the ecclesiastical authorities, but in the last years of his life he gave up his honors, fortune, and profession to become a simple priest. Pia Vogler Jolliffe, DPhil (Linacre College, 2011) responded to the author's discussion of Dr Linacre in the Michaelmas 2015 issue of *Oxford Today* (45–50), in the Trinity 2015 issue. She is Research Fellow at Oxford University's Institute of Population Ageing, Department of Sociology, and is a member of Blackfriars Hall. She wrote (in part):

Dr John Linacre.

> Marlin rightly mentions Linacre's service as physician to the King and founder of the Royal College of Physicians. . . . I was surprised Linacre's Catholic faith was omitted. In fact, he resigned his position as King's physician in 1520 to become a priest.

Calling Linacre a "Catholic" priest, as does the *Catholic Encyclopedia* in its entry on Dr Linacre, could misleadingly create the impression that Linacre became a priest after leaving Henry VIII's service to protest in favor of Rome against his King. But Linacre was loyal to the King, dedicating two pieces of writing to Henry VIII in 1517 and 1519, and he was Cardinal Wolsey's physician as well as the King's. Henry VIII in turn was loyal enough (Defender of the Faith) to Rome during Linacre's lifetime. English Christians were almost all Roman Catholics then; the Lollards and other dissenters within the church had nowhere to go when they were accused of heresy or treason. Not until 1534, when the Pope refused to annul the King's marriage to Catherine, did the split between Henry and the Pope become a schism. Linacre never had to choose between his Pope and his King because he died in 1524, a decade before the schism. That was three years before the King first broached the possibility with Pope Clement VII of annulling his marriage to Catherine of Aragon on the basis that she was previously married to his brother.

20th century Linacre's path to full College status should be of interest to other Permanent Private Halls. Linacre House was founded in 1962 as a non-collegiate, non-residential, multi-disciplinary society, to meet the social needs of graduate students. The first Principal was Mr John Bamborough. Three years later, Linacre House was re-named Linacre College, but without formal college status. In 1977, Linacre moved to Cherwell Edge, formerly the home of a history don, then a Catholic convent, and then a center for graduate students from Oxford colleges. Linacre's new site was opened by Harold Macmillan, then Oxford's Chancellor. The University made Linacre financially independent with a gift of £1 million, because it had become a University priority to create social and residential space for its growing graduate population. Statutes were prepared and in 1986 Linacre College was granted a royal charter as a full college of the University.

Current Head of House Linacre's fourth Principal is Dr Nicholas David (Nick) Brown, a botanist and ecologist. He has been Principal since 2014. He is also a Commonwealth Scholarship Commissioner. Brown was born in Gloucestershire. He completed the International Baccalaureate at UWC Atlantic College in Wales in 1979–1981. He studied geography the University of Cambridge (Churchill College) in 1982–1985 and received an MSc in ecology at the University of Aberdeen. In 1986–1990 he studied for a DPhil in Forest Ecology at the University of Oxford (Linacre College). His thesis was entitled "Dipterocarp regeneration in tropical rain forest gaps of different sizes." He has also completed a diploma in Learning and Teaching in Higher Education. Brown was a lecturer at Manchester University, and in 1992–2010 a lecturer in forestry at Oxford.

Academic and Bumps Standing As a graduate college, Linacre is not ranked in the Norrington Table. But Linacre did have a men's boat and two women's boats in the 2018 Eights Week. The men's eight began at 37th and was bumped twice. The women's first eight began at 20th and got three bumps, to end up at 17th. On overall points, Linacre started and ended in 28th place. But on bumps Linacre came in at 13th place.

LINCOLN COLLEGE

Highlights

- Named for the Bishop of Lincoln, whose See included Oxford.
- The center third of the shield shows the arms of the See.
- On the left (*dexter*) side is the coat of arms of Bishop Fleming.
- On the right (*sinister*) is the coat for Bishop Rotherham.

Arms, Blazon *Tierced in pale First Barry of six Argent and Azure in chief three Lozenges Gules the third Bar charged with a Mullet pierced Sable* (with right foreleg raised), *Second Argent thereon an escutcheon of the Arms of the See of Lincoln ensigned of a Mitre Azure stringed Or* (for the See of Lincoln) *Third Vert three Stags trippant Argent attired Or* (for Rotherham/Scott)

Arms, Origin This form of the blazon dates to the 1574 Visitation by the College of Arms in the person of Richard Lee, Portcullis Pursuivant, on a Visitation to the University. He caused some subsequent controversy by his "boldness" in aggressively confirming the Lincoln arms. Windsor Herald in an email to the author in 2015 cites the official record from the Visitation of 1574 (*Coll. Arms H6.14*) and adds that:

- The lions *passant* on the arms of the See of Lincoln ought to be described as being *in pale*.

- The Mitre is proper; although they are represented predominantly Azure and Or in the record, these are not the only possible tinctures.

- The stags are Or.

The Lincoln College accounts show Richard Lee received 20 shillings for his work. The coat of arms, even though confirmed by three subsequent heraldic visitations, has been displayed inconsistently. The 1574 blazon shows the stags *statant* (all four legs on the ground), whereas Rotherham's authenticated portrait shows them *trippant* (with one front leg up), as well

Detail of Virgin and Child.

as *argent (attired or,* i.e., with only the antlers and hooves *or*). It is also the form of the stags in the Jesus College arms, which, while not granted by the College of Arms, have their own authority by length of use. Components of the arms may have been changed or invented by the impetuous Richard Lee. In 1920 the College of Arms submitted an authoritative coat of arms, modifying what had been in use, and perhaps this should be definitive.

Arms, Nominees Each of the three arms combined in this unusually *tierced per pale* (divided vertically into three parts) shield references the nominees. The blazon is divided into three sections corresponding to the three pales, though a blazon is not properly punctuated or subdivided with numerals: (1) The arms of Richard Fleming, Bishop of Lincoln, who founded the College in 1427. (2) The arms of the See of Lincoln. The corporate designation of the College is "The Warden or Rector and Scholars of the College of the Blessed Mary and All Saints, Lincoln, in the University of Oxford, commonly called Lincoln College." The practice of using an ecclesiastical institution's arms for a founder is frowned on by heraldic authorities. (3) The arms of Thomas Rotherham (also known as Scot de Rotherham), Bishop of Lincoln, later Archbishop of York and Lord High Chancellor of England, who re-endowed the College in 1478.

Arms, Common Variations 1. Below left, unpierced mullet. Should there be a mullet at all? 2. Top, miter at an angle, and the Virgin with with Babe is more *per fesse* than *in chief.* 3. Right, in the Jesus shield, stags are *trippant,* not statant—and *argent attired or,* not *or.*

Why Is the Mullet Pierced? Why Is It There at All? The mullet in the original arms of Bishop Fleming is not pierced, but the one in the college coat arms is. A mistake may have been made in 1574, or earlier, that endures. Brooke-Little, founder of the Heraldry Society and an alumnus of New College, Oxford has commented on the mullet. He served successively as Richmond Herald, Norroy and Ulster King of Arms, and Clarenceux King of Arms; he died in 2006. In his 1951 articles, he says the Lincoln mullet is "probably a cadency mark", though he does not think that it indicated that founder Bishop Fleming was a third son. One version of the Bishop's arms on his portrait has—instead of three lozenges in chief and a pierced mullet—what seems to be a bird *gules* between two roses *gules* and an unpierced mullet. No one knows where the mullet comes from or why it is there. One solution would be to drop it. The other is to leave it mysteriously there, like Fermat's Last Theorem, for future generations to solve.

The Arms of the See of Lincoln (Center Pale) are Improper and Impossible Having three pales in a coat of arms creates complexity. It is also improper to use the arms of a See to represent a college. The personal coat of arms of the founding bishop is more appropriate. These objections apply also to the coats of Corpus Christi and Brasenose. The field of the center pale has sometimes been shown incorrectly as blue (*azure*) rather than silver (*argent*). More

important, multiple versions of the Virgin Mary and Babe have emerged—again, for good reasons! Versions that show a demi-lady (cutting off the lower half of the Virgin and Child) are criticized for their error. But the blazon creates instructions that are almost impossible to carry out legibly. The "Virgin Mary and Babe with Sceptre on a tomb" is actually a Portrait figure, ill-suited for the Landscape space in the "in chief" spot. The Virgin and Child device on the Lincoln and Brasenose arms is overly compressed horizontally in every version I have seen. In this size it is impossible to decipher the device without the blazon. In March 2018, heraldic artist Lee Lumbley tried his hand at making the shield easier to understand, giving more vertical space to the Virgin and Child. An American alumnus of Lincoln, Nelson Ong, has taken an interest in the issue and has raised it with the Rector of Lincoln, Prof. Henry Woudhuysen. Busy though he is, the Rector indicated readiness to consider a revision to the Lincoln arms that meets the tests of

Virgin and Child, See of Lincoln.

heraldic integrity and common sense. The precedent of Merton, which recently updated its arms by eliminating the dexter side (the Saltire) of its shield, may be helpful in moving toward cleaner college arms. Lee Lumbley has contacted a heraldic scholar writing about the arms of the See of Lincoln. They located an early version of the Virgin and Babe shield (above), in Bedford's 1858 book on the Bishops of Lincoln, showing how the Virgin and Child should be portrayed.

Bishop Rotherham's Arms: Trippant or Statant? The Bishop's authenticated portrait in Lincoln's Hall shows three stags *trippant* and *argent* on *vert,* but the College arms show them *statant* and *or.* Brooke-Little showed the disputed stags as *statant* in his 1951 article. The evidence from the portrait suggests that this is an error, a rare one for Brooke-Little.

Similarity to Jesus College Arms An American tourist is said to have entered Lincoln College after the Civil War and asked the porter: "Say, is this Jesus?" To which the porter replied: "You aren't the first person, sir, to confuse Lincoln with Jesus," which the visitor took to be a savvy comment on American politics. The Jesus College arms are blazoned *Vert three stags trippant argent attired or,* which is the same as, or close to, the sinister section of the Lincoln arms. The earliest depiction of the Jesus arms was thought to be about 1590, in a document held by the College of Arms, referring to the stags as having a blue (*azure*) field, but Peter Donoghue, Bluemantle Pursuivant, reports the arms were more likely added 90 years later, on John Speed's 1605 Map of Oxfordshire, with a blue field. The green field first appeared in 1619 in an armorial quarry painted by one of the Van Linge brothers, and was generally used by 1730, although horizontal hatchings (indicating *azure*) were still used on college bookplates as late as 1761. It has been claimed that Jesus stole the three stags from Lincoln, but the counterargument is that the origins of each are distinct. Paul Langford, former Lincoln Rector, has suggested that Jesus College continued the arms adopted by a theological college founded by Rotherham in his home town—Jesus College, Rotherham—which had been suppressed in the time of Edward VI. Another theory is that the stags derive from the arms of Maud Green, Lady Parr, mother of Catherine Parr, last of the six wives of Henry VIII and stepmother to Elizabeth I. The most likely story is that the arms of the College are those of Bishop Rotherham, and John Speed saw them on Lawrence Hall in Ship Street, given to Rotherham in 1476 and leased to Jesus College in 1572. Speed probably assumed the arms to be those of the College when drawing his map in 1605. The Jesus arms

could not be confused with those of Lincoln College, because as of 1574 Lincoln's tierced shield was confirmed by Portcullis Pursuivant.

Lincoln College entrance, from inside.

John Wesley was a Fellow of Lincoln College. He sought to reform the Anglican Church and instead created a new religion, Methodism. Born June 28, 1703 in Epworth, Lincolnshire, England, John was the 15th (!) child of Anglican Rev. Samuel Wesley and his wife Susanna. Samuel was an Oxford graduate and from 1696 on rector of Epworth. Susanna, the 25th (!) child of Samuel Annesley, a Dissenting minister, gave birth to 19 children including John and Charles. She homeschooled all her children to proficiency in Latin, Greek and the Bible. In 1714, at 11, John Wesley was sent to Charterhouse School in London and, in 1720, he matriculated at Christ Church, Oxford, graduating with a B.A. in 1724. He was a year later elected a Fellow of Lincoln College, Oxford. Ordained priest on September 22, 1728, Wesley served the parish for two years, returning to Lincoln in 1729. Meanwhile, John Wesley's younger brother Charles at Christ Church formed a club with two fellow students to study the Christian life. When John returned to Oxford, he became the leader of his brother's group, referred to facetiously as the "Holy Club" and "the Methodists". This evolved into a new religion, of which the Wesley brothers and fellow cleric George Whitefield of Pembroke College are credited with being the founders. John Wesley's core belief was in humanity's utter dependence upon God's grace. John Wesley himself remained during his entire life within the established Anglican church and by the end of his life, he was described as "the best loved man in England".

Current Head of House The Rector since 2012 is Dr Henry Ruxton Woudhuysen, FSA, FBA, who earned his doctorate in Renaissance English literature and was previously Dean of the Faculty of Arts and Humanities at University College London. He earned his DPhil degree from the University of Oxford, in 1981, writing his dissertation on "Leicester's literary patronage: A study of the English court, 1578–1582".

Academic and Bumps Standing The Norrington Table ranks Lincoln 8th on the 2006–16 average, 19th in 2016, 30th in 2017, and 26th in 2018. Lincoln has never been Head of the River. In Eights Week 2018 the first men's eight started at a respectable 19th but was bumped on three of the four days, ending at 22nd. The first women's eight did better, starting in 17th place and bumping on the first day, but ending one down, at 18th. Lincoln had six boats in the water for Eights Week.

MAGDALEN COLLEGE

Highlights

- Founded by William Patten of Waynflete, Bishop of Winchester.
- The lozengy checkerboard is from the Bishop's personal arms.
- The Bishop had headed Winchester and Eton, hence the lilies.
- Magdalen usually rates high academically. It was in 2nd place in 2018.

Arms, Blazon *Lozengy Ermine and Sable (for Patten) on a Chief Sable three Lilies Argent slipped and seeded Or.*

Arms, Origin Ancient. Predates the founding of the College of Arms in 1484.

Arms, Nominee The College is named after Mary Magdalen, but the arms other than the chief are those of the founder, William Patten of Waynflete, Bishop of Winchester and Lord Chancellor. Waynflete was a talented graduate of New College, was ordained, taught at Winchester and served as Provost of Eton. At 50, Henry VI appointed him Bishop of Winchester and Chancellor of England. After Henry's fall, Bishop Waynflete adapted to the Yorkists and continued as bishop till his death at 88. The college arms are those of Waynflete, who derived his heraldic lilies from those of Eton. Magdalen's statutes are largely based on those of New College.

Arms, Meaning Lilies are associated with Eton College, of which Waynflete became Provost. In a 1449 document, King Henry VI described the meaning of lilies in the arms of Eton College: "On a field *sable* three lily-flowers *argent*, intending that Our newly founded College, lasting for ages to come, whose perpetuity We wish to be signified by the stability of the *sable* colour, shall bring forth the brightest flowers redolent of every kind of knowledge, to which also that We may impart something of royal nobility, which may declare the work truly royal and illustrious . . ." The Bishop of Winchester's vision for Magdalen College and choir school cites the same sable field and lilies. Lilies are also symbols of Mary Magdalen. The lozengy pattern of ermine and sable is from the Bishop's personal arms.

Founded 1458 by William Patten of Waynflete, Bishop of Winchester.

MAGDALEN COLLEGE • 51

15th century—William of Waynflete's Dream
Bishop Waynflete of Winchester, son of Richard
Patten (occasionally also referred to as Barbour)
sought to make his college the best in Oxford
and he provided for 40 Fellows and 30 Scholars
(called "Demies" at Magdalen). He had previously served as Master of Winchester (1429–42)
and Provost of Eton from 1443 on. Following
the New College model, he provided for a large
permanent choir, one of only four colleges
at Oxford with such choirs written into their
foundation. The Magdalen College choir school
became the Magdalen College School. The
Bishop lived on for more than a quarter-century after he founded the college and he made
sure that Magdalen had a fine chapel and other
buildings, and proper statutes.

16th century—Royal Support Royal visitors
included popular Edward IV and usurper Richard III. The founder of Christ Church, Cardinal
Thomas Wolsey, was one of two cardinals to
have spent time at Magdalen; Wolsey was there
as a Fellow. Wolsey became young Henry VIII's
chief minister for two decades, but fell out of
favor when he failed to obtain papal approval
for Henry's divorcing Catherine of Aragon.

17th century—The Civil War Magdalen, like
many other colleges at Oxford, suffered from
the religious-based Civil War of the 1640s. All
of Oxford except Merton supported Charles I.
The Reformation was opposed to lavish orna-
mentation in Roman Catholic churches, and
the austere Roundheads (so-called because
they opposed the wigs and curls of the High
Anglican Cavaliers) disapproved of continuing
use of images in Anglican churches. The beautiful Magdalen College chapel suffered tragic
vandalism during this period. When Charles I
was rousted out of his hiding places in Oxford
by Oliver Cromwell's Army, Magdalen's President and many Fellows were purged.

17th century—Contretemps with James II
Cromwell failed to install a Republic. After
his death, Charles II was installed during the

Restoration. In 1687, after Magdalen's President
died, James II tried twice to force the Fellows to
accept a President of his choosing. The Fellows
refused, and James demanded that all those who
opposed him be expelled. This caused national
outrage. Late in 1688, James II reinstated the
expelled Fellows. However, public opinion
had turned and it was too late to save the king;
before the end of the year he was replaced in the
"Glorious Revolution" by William III of Orange.
The defeat of James II is celebrated every year at
Magdalen.

*Magdalen Tower, dating from 1492,
viewed from High Street.*

**20th century—The College Revived in the
20th Century.** Under Frederick Bulley and—
even more—Sir Herbert Warren, the College's
reputation grew. Under Warren in 1912 the
then Prince of Wales (later Edward VIII), came
up to the College. With the support of Bulley
and Warren, the Chapel Choir also improved
greatly, attaining the national reputation that
it still holds. The 20th century saw Magdalen's
academic reputation burnished by two famed
Fellows, theologian and writer C. S. Lewis
and historian A. J. P. Taylor. Women were first
admitted in 1979.

Current Head of House The President since
2005 is Sir David Charles Clary, FRS. Born
in Halesworth, Suffolk, he attended Colches-
ter Royal Grammar School in 1964–71 and
earned a BSc (1974) from the University of
Sussex and a PhD (1977) and ScD (1997) from

the University of Cambridge, Corpus Christi College. In 1996, he was director of the Centre for Theoretical and Computational Chemistry and professor at University College London. In 2002, he moved to Oxford, where he headed the Division of Mathematical and Physical Sciences and was professorial fellow of St John's College. In 2009–2013 he was the first chief scientific adviser to the Foreign and Commonwealth Office.

Academic and Bumps Standing Magdalen is usually at or near the top on both measures. It was first academically in the Norrington Table in 2015 and its 2006–2016 average was the best among the colleges. It was 3rd in 2016, fell to 11th in 2017, and recovered to 2nd place in 2018. Magdalen has been Head of the River 20 times since intercollegiate Eights were started in 1815. It was Head of the River between 2004 and 2007. In 2018, however, the Magdalen first men's eight was bumped in Summer Eights every day for four days and it fell from ninth to 13th, while much smaller Trinity's first eight had three bumps and climbed to 10th place. Magdalen's first women's boat was bumped once and fell from 8th to 9th place.

MANSFIELD COLLEGE

Highlights

- Founded in Birmingham, became first Nonconformist college at Oxford in 1886.
- The coat of arms emphasizes evangelical Christianity and direct access to the word of God.
- Buildings include many representations of Oliver Cromwell and other dissidents.
- Mansfield's religious tradition is evident, but since 1955 has diminished.

Arms, Blazon *Gules an open Book proper inscribed DEUS LOCUTUS EST NOBIS IN FILIO in letters Sable bound Argent edged and clasped Or between three Cross crosslets Gold.*

Arms, Origin Granted 10 Feb 1956.

Arms, Meaning The red (*gules*) field signifies England, the book is clearly the Bible, and the meaning of the Latin words, "God has spoken to us through His Son", is that since God speaks to us directly through Jesus in the Bible, we do not have to rely on an Established Church to interpret for us. The three cross crosslets are Christian symbols of worldwide evangelism. They may each be seen as four Latin crosses at right angles, pointed in four directions. These four directions may be interpreted as the points of a compass, "the four corners of the world", or the four evangelists. The cross crosslets may reference the arms of Richard de Beauchamp, Earl of Warwick, as Birmingham was formerly in Warwickshire.

Founders George and Elizabeth Mansfield and Elizabeth's sister Sarah Glover were Birmingham residents with no heirs and an interest in promoting a learned clergy in their Nonconforming congregation. They were the principal donors to the original Spring Hill College in 1838.

19th century The college was founded originally as Spring Hill College as an independent college for Nonconformist students in

Birmingham, who could not work toward a degree at a university. Until 1871, students who did not conform to the Church of England could attend universities but were forbidden by law from obtaining a degree. In 1871, the Universities Tests Act ended all religious tests for non-theological degrees at Oxford, Cambridge, London and Durham Universities. The Prime Minister who championed these reforms, William Ewart Gladstone, encouraged creation of a Nonconformist college at Oxford; Spring Hill College responded by moving itself to Oxford in 1886. Renamed Mansfield College, it was the first Nonconformist college to open in Oxford, though it would take many decades for it to be on the same footing as the existing colleges. The main Victorian building was designed by architect Basil Champneys, and was built in 1887–1889. The first Principal, in 1886–1909, was Andrew Martin Fairbairn, whose formal education was limited, but of whom Lord Acton said "no man in Oxford was more learned".

20th century Initially the college accepted male students only, the first woman being admitted in 1913. Mansfield admitted its first mixed-sex cohort in 1979, having previously not accepted women for degrees. During World War II, more than 40 members of staff from Government Code & Cypher School moved to the college to prepare the British codes and cyphers. In 1955, the college was granted the status of Permanent Private Hall within the University of Oxford and in 1995 a Royal Charter was awarded giving the institution full college status. Since 1955, its Nonconformist aspects have gradually diminished. Until 2007, the United Reformed Church (URC) sponsored a course at Mansfield for training ordinands. The Nonconformist history of the college is however still apparent with portraits of Oliver Cromwell and other dissenters in the Senior Common Room, Hall and college chapel. Chapel services are still conducted in a Nonconformist tradition.

Current Head of House The Principal since 2018 is Helen Mountfield, QC, a British barrister and legal scholar, specialising in administrative, human rights, and education law. She was a founding member in 2000 of Matrix Chambers, from which she still practices. She has been a Deputy High Court Judge since 2013. She has co-authored seven editions of *Blackstone's Guide to the Human Rights Act 1998*.

Mansfield College tie in use.

Academic and Bumps Standing The Norrington Table ranked Mansfield 29th of 37 colleges (including PPHs) in 2006–2016. They were 31st in 2016. Excluding the PPHs, Mansfield was 14th in 2017, 20th in 2018. The Mansfield College Boat Club is popular at the College. The first men's eight ranked 17th in the beginning of 2018 Summer Eights and the first women's eight ranked 16th. They were both bumped on three days. On points, Mansfield fell from 18th to 20th. Its four crews ranked 35th on bumps, negative 13. Being a small college, Mansfield had difficulty covering some sports and has therefore combined in partnership with Merton College for sports such as rugby games.

MERTON COLLEGE

Highlights

- Founded by Walter de Merton, Bishop of Rochester
- Merton was the only Parliamentary College at Oxford
- Queen Henrietta Maria stayed at Merton during the Siege
- Merton ranks near the top academically, was 4th in 2018.

Arms, Blazon *Or three Chevronels per pale Azure and Gules the centre one counter-changed.*

Arms, Origin Ancient. Predates the College of Arms, founded in 1484.

Arms, Meaning The Merton College arms are those of its founder, Walter de Merton, Lord Chancellor under Henry III and Edward I, and Bishop of Rochester. The first and third chevronels are "per pale" (stacked vertically) blue (*azure*) and red (*gules*), with the middle one counter-changed (colours reversed). Motto (not shown): "Let he who fears God do good deeds." The arms used to be shown often impaled with those of the See of Rochester, but Merton College has thought better of this and thereby wins both aesthetically and heraldically.

Founded 1264 by Walter de Merton (c. 1205–1277), Lord Chancellor and Bishop of Rochester.

13th century—Foundation of Merton The "House of Scholars of Merton" originally had properties in Surrey as well as in Oxford. Not until the mid-1260s did Walter de Merton acquire the core of the present site in Oxford, on the south side of St John's Street (renamed Merton Street). The college was consolidated on this site by 1274, when Walter made his final revisions to the college statutes. His first acquisition of property included the parish church of St John (used for the chapel) and three houses to the east that now form the north side of Front Quad.

Walter obtained permission from the king to extend these properties south to the old city wall to form a square site. The college continued to acquire other properties as they became available. At one time, the college owned all the land from boundary of what is now Christ Church to the southeastern corner of the city. (The western end was leased in 1515 to create Corpus Christi.)

13th century—Oldest College? Merton's claim to be the oldest college in Oxford is based on its being the first to achieve a full community of scholars. Balliol College and University College had other features of a college, but Merton was the first college to achieve academic goals and the first to be provided with "statutes" governing the college. Merton's statutes date back to 1264, whereas neither Balliol nor University College had statutes until the 1280s.

14th century—Mob Quad at Merton was built in the 14th century and is sometimes called the oldest quadrangle of any Oxford or Cambridge college, but Merton's own Front Quad was enclosed earlier and other colleges, for example Corpus Christi College, Cambridge, have older quads. The old library occupies the upper floor of the south and west ranges of Mob Quad, and the original archive room is still in the north east corner.

17th century—Home of the Queen in the Civil War Merton's buildings were commandeered by the Royalists when they made

Oxford their capital. Merton housed much of Charles I's Catholic court. This included the King's French wife, Queen Henrietta Maria, who was housed near what is now the Queen's Room, above the arch between Front and Fellows' Quads. A portrait of Charles I hangs near the Queen's Room as a reminder of the role it played.

17th century—Sympathy with Parliament
Merton was the only Oxford college to side with Parliament during the English Civil War. Merton's Warden Nathaniel Brent was an amazing survivor of the religious wars:

- The Visitor of Merton in 1638 was the autocratic Catholic William Laud (1573–1645), five years into his post as Archbishop of Canterbury. Laud wrote to Warden Brent insisting on major reforms.

- Brent, who had previously been Vicar-General to Laud, was displeased. When in 1640 Charles I reconvened Parliament to pay Scottish military bills, Parliament arrested Laud for treasonous opposition to Calvinist beliefs, and Brent testified against Laud at his trial in 1644.

- Laud was executed in January 1645. The pun "give great praise to the Lord, and little Laud to the devil" was advice to King Charles from Archibald Armstrong, the court jester. (Laud was known to be touchy about being short.)

- However . . . Savilian Astronomy Professor John Greaves, a Merton Sub-Warden, grieved at Laud's death and circulated a petition complaining about Warden Brent's testimony.

- So Warden Brent was deposed by Charles I in January 1646 and replaced by William Harvey.

- But the worm turned again. Thomas Fairfax captured Oxford for the Parliamentarians after its third siege in 1646. Brent returned to Oxford in 1647 as president of visitors charged by Parliament to correct "offences, abuses, and disorders" at the University.

- So Brent accused Greaves of misappropriating Merton's plate and funds for King Charles. In 1648, Greaves lost his Merton fellowship and his Savilian chair! Winner: Brent.

Merton College arms on gate.

20th century—The Time Ceremony Students dressed in formal academic dress walk backwards around the Fellows' Quad, drinking port. They once also held candles. Many students now link arms and twirl around at each corner of the quad. The purported function of this activity is to maintain the integrity of the space-time continuum during the transition from British Summer Time to Greenwich Mean Time, which occurs in the early hours of the last Sunday in October. The ceremony was invented by two undergraduates in 1971 to spoof other Oxford ceremonies and societies. The original celebration was of the end of the one-year experimental period of British Standard Time in 1968–1971, when the UK first stayed one hour ahead of GMT. Associated with the ceremony are the toasts "To good old times!" and "Long live the counter-revolution!" Merton is the only Oxford college in Oxford to hold a triennial *winter* ball, most recently in 2016.

21st century—Admissions, by Race and Gender In 2010, it was falsely reported that Merton had not admitted a black student in the previous five years. The University reported that Merton had admitted at least one black undergraduate since 2005. A University spokeswoman said that black students tended to apply for particularly oversubscribed subjects. Merton admitted its first female students in 1980 and was the second formerly male college to elect a female head of house, in 1994. Since 2007, all Merton accommodation is now mixed by gender and course.

Current Head of House The Warden since 2010 is Sir Martin John Taylor, a British mathematician and academic. He was professor of mathematics at the School of Mathematics, University of Manchester. He was previously a don at Trinity College, Cambridge, having earned his BA at Pembroke College, Oxford and his PhD at King's College, London. Taylor was born in Leicester and educated at Wyggeston Grammar School.

Academic and Rowing Standing Since the introduction in 2004 of an official Norrington Table published by the University, Merton has occupied one of the top three positions every year (often coming in 1st) until 2012, when it dropped to 14th. In 2014, it regained the 1st position, preserving its status as one of the most academically successful colleges of the last 20 years. Merton ranked 2nd on the 2006–2016 average. It was 1st again in 2016, 2nd in 2017, and 4th in 2018. It is not so dominant on the water, however, in the history of Eights, it was Head of the River only once, in 1951. In 2018, its first men's eight started at 24th place and had three bumps, ending in 21st. Its first women's boat started in 26th place and was bumped three times. The overall point score for Summer Eights moved Merton up from a combined rank of 24th to 23rd.

NEW COLLEGE

Highlights

- Founded by William of Wykeham, who created Winchester to prepare boys for New College.
- The first non-Wykehamist was William Spooner, famed for comically transposing initial letters of words.
- New College rates #5 on the Norrington Table in August 2018.
- Why the New College Boat Club uses royal Swedish colors

Arms, Blazon *Argent two Chevronels Sable between three Roses Gules barbed and seeded proper* (for Wykeham).

Arms, Origin Ancient. Predates the College of Arms, founded in 1484.

Arms, Meaning The arms of New College are those of the founder, William de Wykeham, Bishop of Winchester, who was born in Wickham, Hampshire. It was called "New" College to distinguish it from Oriel, also named contemporaneously for St Mary. The first chevron indicates that the Bishop was an architect,

responsible for a tower at Windsor Castle and for the major part of Winchester Cathedral. Chevrons and chevronels are interpreted as rafters or set-squares and suggest a mason or architect. The second chevron is said to have been added when Wykeham became Bishop, which would have been one of the earliest examples of multiple chevrons indicating rank. The red roses predate claims by the Rosicrucians that they reference Wykeham's having attained the Grade of Philosophus in their order in 1357. Wykeham's motto was "Manners Makyth Man", which continues to be the motto of Winchester College and New College.

He assumed this motto along with his coat of arms. He was the subject of a biography by Bishop Lowth and was mentioned in sketches by Lord Brougham, in his *Old England's Worthies* (1857), and by Froissart.

Founded 1379 by William of Wykeham, to train priests in the wake of the widespread deaths from plagues. The first women were admitted in 1979, exactly 600 years later.

14th century—New College and Winchester College Wykeham obtained a royal charter for New College in 1379 and it opened its doors in 1386. He also procured both a royal license and a papal bull to found the Winchester College grammar school in 1394, to provide good students for New College. Wykeham was motivated by the mid-14th century Black Death, which killed more than half of Europe's population and 20 percent of Britain's, and left behind a dearth or priests. New College and Winchester were both the work of master mason William Wynford. The pleasing array of buildings at New College is a testament to him, and to Wykeham's management skills and the lavish incomes from his many church positions.

14th century—William of Wykeham Wykeham survived the roller-coaster era of 14th-century English history, which ended the careers or lives of others with weaker survival skills. Born William Longe in Wykeham, Hampshire, he was educated at a grammar school in Winchester and served as a chaplain until 1349, when his talent was discovered by the King. Assigned first to supervising building trades at Winchester Castle, he was promoted to doing architectural work for the King that won him renown and in 1361 the post of secretary for finance. He was ordained priest in 1362 and received generous emoluments. Pope Urban V made him Bishop of Winchester in 1367 and soon after, Edward III made him Chancellor of England, then Britain's highest civil office. However, conflict with France

resumed in 1369, and the King needed money. Wykeham failed to raise enough and was in the doghouse, resigning as Chancellor in 1371. As Edward III aged, William prudently maintained ties with the Earl of March, which helped when his successor as Chancellor, William, 4th Baron Latimer, was impeached. Through March, Wykeham became one of four bishops appointed to the new royal council in 1376. Alas, his friendship with Lord March distressed John of Gaunt, who had supported Latimer. So, when Latimer was pardoned by Edward III in October 1376, Wykeham was found guilty of a financial irregularity and was banished from court, his incomes from church properties being seized in late 1376. After Edward III died, Wykeham was pardoned by the new king, Richard II, and served again as Chancellor in 1389–1391. When Henry IV deposed Richard II in 1399, Wykeham maneuvered to welcome him in Winchester in 1400. William went to his well-earned rest in 1404 at Bishop's Waltham in Hampshire. He had become one of the richest men in England.

14th century—The Making of Wykeham When invited to supervise the building of Windsor Castle, Wykeham supervised a crew of more than 350 masons and related trades. The story is widely told that, upon the wall of Windsor Castle's Winchester tower was inscribed HOC FECIT WYKEHAM ("This made Wykeham"). Edward III was offended at Wykeham's claiming all the credit for the tower, at which point Wykeham cleverly explained that the inscription should be interpreted as noting that the building of the castle was "the making" of the architect.

15th century—First Founder-Written Statutes Wykeham was the first person to draw up the statutes of the college he founded. It took him 13 years, but in 1403, the year before he died, Wykeham presented the final statutes. New College was the first to pair a school (Winchester) with an Oxbridge college, and was the model for Eton and King's College (New

College's sister college in Cambridge). New College was the first college in Oxford to be designed around a main quadrangle. It was also the first Oxford college for undergraduates and the first to have senior members of the college give tutorials.

19th century—William Archibald Spooner (1844–1930) was a don and Warden at New College for 60 years, notable for his absent-mindedness, and tendency to transpose initial letters or syllables while speaking, with unintentionally comic effect. Spooner was born in London and was educated at Oswestry School and New College, where he was the first non-Wykehamist to become an undergraduate in the nearly 480 years of New College's existence. He lectured on ancient history and philosophy (especially on Aristotle's *Ethics*). Spooner was considered kindly, hospitable, and devoted to scholarship and duty. His appearance was reminiscent of Mr. Magoo, as his eyesight was poor and his head was large relative to his body. Some Spoonerisms:

- "The weight of rages will press hard upon the employer."
- "The next hymn will be Kinkering Congs" (Conquering Kings).
- "You have hissed all my mystery lectures, and were caught fighting a liar in the quad. Having tasted two worms, you will leave by the next town drain". (You have missed all my history lectures, and were caught lighting a fire in the quad. Having wasted two terms, you will leave by the next down train.)

Spooner is supposed to have invited a don to tea, "to welcome Stanley Casson, our new archaeology Fellow". "But, sir," the man protested, "I *am* Stanley Casson". "Never mind," Spooner said, "Come all the same."

Current Head of House The Warden since 2016 is Peter Miles Young. Previously he spent his entire career with Ogilvy & Mather, serving until 2016 as its worldwide Chairman and CEO. He retains a non-executive role with the firm. He was educated at Bedford School and at New College, Oxford, where he read Modern History.

Colours of the King of Sweden granted to New College rowers.

Academic and Rowing Standing New College ranked 3rd in the Norrington Table for the 2006–16 average. It came in 18th in 2016, 1st in 2017 (unless you count Wycliffe Hall, a Permanent Private Hall that had a freakishly good year with just five firsts and four upper seconds). In 2018, New College ranked 5th among the 30 colleges.

New College has a unique place in Oxford sporting history. In 1912, the New College Boat Club sent its 1st eight to the Summer Olympics in Stockholm, Sweden, to represent Great Britain. The other British crew was the Leander crew, composed mostly of Magdalen rowers, headed by Magdalen's captain. The two British crews were the favourites for gold. They defeated their competitors and were both in the final. The course in Stockholm had one less-favoured lane, requiring the cox to steer around a protruding boathouse and then back under a bridge. Before the final, the two British captains met to toss for lanes. New College won the toss and following gentlemanly tradition offered the choice of lanes to their opponents, who were expected by tradition, in gentlemanly fashion, to refuse this offer. However the Leander/Magdalen captain accepted the offer and chose the better lane. Leander went on to win the gold medal, leaving New

College with the silver. King Gustav V of Sweden was so distressed at the impropriety of this ungentlemanly conduct that he presented his colours to New College. Ever since, New College rowers have raced in the purple and gold of the royal house of Sweden. The toast is: "God damn bloody Magdalen!"—quoting the New College stroke Robert Bourne as he crossed the finish line. The abbreviation "GDBM" is still on the bottom of the New College Boat Club (NCBC) letterhead. NCBC is also one of the few Oxford clubs to have held both headships at Summer Eights, though not in the same year. New College's men's eight has been Head of the River 16 times since the intercollegiate races began, most recently in 1986. The first eight was bumped twice in 2018, falling from 12th to 14th. Its women's eight has been Head of the River twice, most recently in 2005. In 2018 the women's eight was promising, making a bump every day and rising from 11th to 7th place. Overall, on points, New College jumped two places in 2018, from 11th to 9th place.

NUFFIELD COLLEGE

Highlights

- The College's arms are those of its able founder, Lord Nuffield.

- He was Britain's leading car-maker in the 1910s and 1920s.

- The college is for graduate students only.

- Its architecture, especially the tower, has been criticized.

- Its ongoing research programmes have broken new ground.

Arms, Blazon *Ermine on a Fesse Or between in chief two Roses Gules barbed and seeded proper and in base a Balance of the second three Pears Sable* (for Nuffield).

Arms, Origin Granted 5 May 1958.

Arms, Meaning The arms are those of the 1937 founder, William Morris, auto maker, who lived in Nuffield, South Oxfordshire, and was named baronet, baron, and later Viscount Nuffield. The red roses are for England. The black pears are for the City of Worcester where he was born; Queen Elizabeth I by legend saw them growing ripe and unpicked and suggested they be put on the city's coat of arms. The scales are for his motto, *Fiat Justitia* [*, et Pereat Mundus*]–"let justice be done" ["though the world perish"], a motto used by Emperor Ferdinand I.

Founded in 1937 after a donation to the University by the Lord Nuffield, founder of Morris Motors.

20th century—Lord Nuffield was called by *The Times* in 1949 "the greatest benefactor of [Oxford] University since the Middle Ages". William Morris, later Lord Nuffield, was born in 1877, left school at 15, and worked in Oxford as a repairer and maker of bicycles, then of motor cycles and finally of cars. He was one of Britain's first factory owners to use mass production methods. His company, Morris Motors Ltd, prospered greatly in 1910s and 1920s. The Morris Oxford of 1913, the post-war Morris Minor and the MG cars became world-famous. Lord Nuffield was made a baron in 1934, and a viscount in 1938, and took the name of Nuffield, the Oxfordshire village where he settled. Lord Nuffield remained personally frugal despite his wealth and devoted all his energies to his philanthropic work. The Nuffield Foundation, his largest benefaction, was founded in 1943 with a gift of £10 million of shares in his company. He died in 1963.

Morris Oxford was originally a bicycle shop.

20th century—Nuffield Firsts Nuffield College claims to be the first college at Oxford to have both women and men housed together, and the first to accept both men and women. It was the first to consist solely of graduate students. It was the first in modern times to have a defined subject focus, namely the social sciences. (Some of these firsts may conflict with claims at other colleges such as Linacre.)

21st century—The Nuffield College Endowment Nuffield is one of Oxford's smallest colleges, with some 75 postgraduate students and 60 academic fellows. It is a graduate college specialising in the social sciences, particularly economics, politics and sociology. The College's endowment in mid-2015 was £180 million($239 million) or £2.4 million ($3.2 million) per student, of which the unrestricted endowment was the major portion. It is reported on Wikipedia to be the wealthiest educational institution per student in the world, which cannot be true. It is far less than Rockefeller University in Manhattan, with 200 students and $2 billion endowment, $10 million per student. It is more than Princeton University's overall endowment of $2.8 million/student but less than its more comparable Institute for Advanced Study with 200 students and a $750+ million endowment ($3.75 million per student). It is certainly true to say

that Nuffield is well-endowed, able to attract the best and brightest students in its fields of interest.

20th century—The Controversial Tower Nuffield's architecture is designed to conform to the traditional college quadrangle layout. The architect Austen Harrison's first design was rejected by Nuffield as "un-English". Some feel that this first design was a missed opportunity, the greatest "architectural casualty" of the decade. Harrison's redesign was approved in 1940, with construction delayed by the Second World War and then by the building boom; it was not completed until 1960. The tower was planned to be ornamental but was redesigned to hold the college's library. It was the first tower built in Oxford for 200 years and is about 150 feet tall, including the flèche at the top. The modernist tower is the College's dominant feature and has been criticized as an "ungainly" masonry-clad steel-framed bookstack. The windows do look a bit like the boxes on a Hollerith card. Architectural historian Sir Nikolaus Pevsner defended the tower, hailing a new Oxford landmark that in time would "be loved". But Sir Simon Jenkins despaired of this Pollyannish forecast and argued for "vegetation" (ivy) as the tower's "best hope".

21st century—Research Innovation The College is home today to significant research programmes like:

- The Centre for Social Investigation, an interdisciplinary research group examining inequalities and social progress in Britain. Nuffield's major programme of research on Social Mobility in Britain has been widely noted.

- The Nuffield Election Studies programme, source of some major research developments in social science. It was the birthplace of the "Oxford School" of Industrial Relations. It pioneered cost-benefit analysis in developing countries and it made a major contribution to econometrics.

Current Head of House The Warden since 2012 is Sir Andrew William Dilnot, CBE, formerly Director of the Institute for Fiscal Studies in 1991–2002. He was Principal of St Hugh's College in 2002–2012, when he was the only Head of House educated at a comprehensive school. He served as Chair of the UK Statistics Authority in 2012–2017. Born in Swansea, Dilnot attended Olchfa School and read PPE at St John's College, Oxford. Dilnot was a presenter on BBC Radio 4's programme about statistics, *More or Less* and co-authored The Tiger That Isn't, based on the programme. In 2005 he became an Oxford Pro Vice-Chancellor.

Academic and Rowing Standing Nuffield is for graduate students only and therefore is not in the Norrington Table. Unlike Wolfson, which filled seven boats (three men's and four women's!), Nuffield did not compete under its own banner on the river and instead provided rowers (and captains) for the Linacre boat. Nuffield's website observes that it has been providing most of the rowers and leadership of the Linacre boat. The Linacre men's boat started in 37th place in 2018 and was bumped twice. The Linacre women's eight did much better in 2018, starting in 20th place and getting three bumps.

ORIEL COLLEGE

Highlights

- Oriel College was the first founded by a monarch
- Three lions passant are the oldest symbol of English royalty
- Oriel was at the center of religious battles
- Today it excels both on the river and in examinations

Arms, Blazon *Gules three Lions passant guardant in pale Or a Border engrailed Argent.*

Arms, Origin Ancient. Predates the College of Arms, founded in 1484.

Arms, Meaning The three lions passant guardant are the oldest symbol of English royalty, from the time of William I the Conqueror, who used the Norman two-lion coat. The College, the first founded directly by a monarch, uses the arms of Edward II, i.e., the three gold lions of the Plantagenets on a red background. The College is differenced by an engrailed silver border.

Arms, Nominee Who is the Nominee? The College uses the arms of Edward II. But it was originally named at its foundation in 1326 "the College of the Blessed Virgin Mary". Its nickname has to do with a property given soon

after foundation, "La Oriole". Two contemporary new colleges were named after Mary. To avoid confusion, one got called New College. The other got called Oriel. Why Oriel? That's another story, below.

Founded 24 April 1324, when the Rector of the University Church, Adam de Brome, obtained a licence from King Edward II to create a "college of scholars" studying subjects "in honour of the Virgin", budgeting £30 a year for a Provost and ten Fellows. To fund the budget with rents, in 1324 Brome bought three properties. Not until the 16th century did Oriel admit undergraduates.

Unusual Oriel Insignia The College colours are *two white stripes on navy*, used on oar blades and clothing (Trinity uses three white stripes). The College has an unusual variety of other formal insignia including the badge of the Tortoise Club and the The Prince of Wales's feathers on college buildings, the official College tie and the Boat Club Blazer. The feathers probably represent Edward, the Black Prince, Prince of Wales, eldest grandson of Edward II; possibly they represent ill-fated Charles I.

14th century—Oldest Royal College, 1324

The prior claim by University College that it was founded by King Alfred (849–899) has been relinquished in the opening lines of University College's self-description, leaving Oriel as the oldest royal foundation. Founded by Adam de Brome under the patronage of Edward II, it was originally named the Hall of the Blessed Mary at Oxford. Oriel was the fifth college to be founded at Oxford. The reigning British monarch is Oriel College's official Visitor.

14th century—Origin of the Name Oriel,

1329 Under royal patronage, Brome tapped revenues of the University Church to Oriel, in return for the College's staffing daily church services. In 1329, Edward III granted the College a large house known as "La Oriole" on the site of what is now First or Front Quad. Since then, the College acquired its nickname Oriel, referencing the oriel window of this house and providing a differentiation from New College, which was also dedicated to Mary. An oriel window is an upper-floor version of a bay window. It projects out from the wall to let in light and gain a greater latitude of view, and adds a pleasing feature to the exterior wall.

15th century—Support for Wycliffe's Lollardy

In the early 1410s several Fellows of Oriel took to the streets to protest Archbishop Arundel's sanctions against Lollardy, i.e., the belief that salvation came through personal faith and good works and not through Church sacraments or adherence to Roman doctrine. (The Roman Catholic principle was *extra ecclesiam nulla salus*, no salvation except through the Church.) Its

Oxford-based proponent, John Wyclif (also spelled Wycliffe), had been Master of Balliol. Disregarding the Provost's support of the Archbishop, Oriel Fellows fought bloody battles with other scholars, killing one of the Chancellor's servants when they attacked his house.

17th century—Royal Defenders, 1643

A general obligation was imposed on Oxford colleges to support the Royalist cause in the English Civil War. Almost all of Oriel's plate was given, including more than 29 lb. of gilt and more than 52 lb. of white plate. The College was assessed 1/40 of the weekly sum of £40 charged to the colleges and halls to fortify the city. When the Oxford Parliament was assembled at Christ Church in 1644, Oriel housed the Executive Committee of the Privy Council.

17th century—Civil War among the Fellows,

1673 James Davenant, a Fellow since 1661, complained in 1673 to the Bishop of Lincoln about the election of Thomas Twitty as a Fellow. The Bishop appointed a commission that included the Dean of Christ Church. Based on Dean Fell's report, the Bishop decreed that a majority (quorum) of Fellows should always be present at an election and Fellows should be admitted immediately after their election. These were good election reforms.

Oriel College, showing oriel window.

19th century—Noetics and Tractarians Oriel led Oxford reforms of academic standards and religious revival. Oriel Fellowships were opened to competitive examination at the end of the 18th century, bringing many great names. As a result, in the early 19th century, the College became the centre of the "Oriel Noetics" led by clerical liberals such as Fellows Richard Whately and Thomas Arnold. During the 1830s, two eminent Fellows of Oriel, John Keble and John Henry Newman, supported by Canon Edward Pusey (initially an Oriel Fellow, later at Christ Church), led the Oxford Movement, also known as Tractarians or Puseyites. Disappointed in the complacent Church of England of its day, the group sought to rekindle the passion of the early Christians. Provost Edward Hawkins was their determined opponent. Above the entrance to the chapel is a small oriel that, until the 1880s, was part of a suite, used by Richard Whately as a pantry and later by John Henry Newman as a place of prayer. When the organ was installed in 1884, the space was used for the blower. In 1991 this space was rebuilt as a memorial to Newman and the Oxford Movement.

20th century—The 'Ole, WWI During the Great War, Somerville College was used as a military hospital. The young women who were displaced were billeted on Oriel. So a wall was built dividing Third Quad from Second Quad to separate them from the Oriel men. Vera Brittain, one of the Somerville students, recalled in her autobiography, *Testament of Youth*:

> [T]he few remaining undergraduates in the still masculine section of Oriel not unnaturally concluded that it would be a first-rate "rag" to break down the wall which divided them from the carefully guarded young females in St. Mary Hall. Great perturbation filled the souls of the Somerville dons when they came down to breakfast one morning to find that a large gap had suddenly appeared in the protecting masonry, through which had been thrust a hilarious placard: "OO MADE THIS 'ERE 'OLE?" "MICE!!!"

For the next 24 hours, members of the Senior Common Room, including the Principal, took turns sitting by the hole, to prevent any Thisbe from accessing an Oriel Pyramus on the other side.

20th century–Admission of Women, 1985 Despite their WWI eagerness to break down the wall separating men from women, Oriel was the last all-male college in Oxford to admit women as undergraduates. In 1984, the Senior Common Room voted 23–4 to admit women starting from 1986, but the Junior Common Room president protested: "The distinctive character of the college will be undermined".

21st century–Must Rhodes Fall? By Oriel's 685th anniversary, nearly 50 Fellows, 300 undergraduates and 200 graduate students were looking forward to celebrating Oriel's 700th anniversary in 2026. But the College was challenged in January 2016 by the Rhodes Must Fall campaign, demanding removal of a statue of Cecil Rhodes, the College's most important benefactor. He was a man with moral blind spots by today's standards, but was an admired builder of the British Empire that lives on as the British Commonwealth. The Provost created a group to study the proposal. Alumni donors wrote in that they would end approximately £100 million in regular giving or pledges if the College removed the statue. The chair of the Commons Select Committee on Education told the Provost to reconsider her ambivalence. Meanwhile, the College was preparing to reduce staff. As of 2018, the statue is still in place and meanwhile the College and University have a clearer idea of what many of their alumni care about and how they can express their views.

Current Head of House The Provost since 2013 is Moira Wallace, OBE, the first female Provost. She was previously in 2008–2012 the first Permanent Secretary of the Department of Energy and Climate Change. Before that she was Director General of the Crime Reduction and Community Safety Group in the Home Office. Before that Wallace was ten years in HM Treasury, including three years as Private Secretary to Nigel Lawson and John Major when each was Chancellor of the Exchequer.

Academic and Rowing Standing Oriel was first place in the 16 Norrington Table until a *savant* made an adjustment, knocking it to second place, with Merton at the top. The 2006–16 average rank was 19th, and in 2017 Oriel fell back to 21st. In 2018, Oriel ranked 12th out of 30 colleges. Oriel's record on the river is a lot more consistent. Sharing a boathouse opposite Christ Church Meadow with Lincoln and Queen's, Oriel has in recent years been celebrating victories. It holds more head-of-the-river wins in Torpids (the winter intercollegiate races) than any other college, winning a double headship (men's and women's) in 2006 and again in 2018. Oriel's

prowess dates back at least to 1842, when it bumped Trinity to become Head of the River. During 7th week in Trinity Term, the Oriel Boat Club hosts an annual Regatta. Oriel's Tortoise Club (made up of 1st Summer Eight and 1st Torpid crews, including coxes) has its own badge, formalized in a grant by Letters Patent dated 20 April 2009, and signed by the three Kings of Arms. The badge is blazoned: *A Tortoise displayed the shell circular Azure charged with two concentric annulets Argent.* The Oriel Boat Club blazer is unusual—ivory with navy blue piping and cuff rings, bearing the three-ostrich-feather emblem on the breast-pocket patch. In the 2018 Summer Eights, Oriel's first men's eight started in 3rd place and bumped Christ Church, ending 2nd behind Keble. The Oriel first women's eight started in 14th place and had three bumps, ending in 11th place. On overall points, Oriel rose from 7th to 5th place.

PEMBROKE COLLEGE

Highlights

- Rampant lions from the Founder, the Earl of Pembroke
- Rose and Thistle for James I of England, VI of Scotland
- Pembroke is "More Shire than Mordor" (*Lord of the Rings*)
- One of the top colleges in intercollegiate rowing.

Arms, Blazon *Per pale Azure and Gules three Lions rampant Argent* (for Hubert) *in a Chief party per pale Argent and Or, in the first a Rose Gules* (for England)*, in second a Thistle of Scotland proper.*

Arms, Origin The Grant of Arms from the College of Heralds to Pembroke College is dated 14 February 1625 and signed by Richard St. George, Clarenceux King of Arms.

Arms, Meaning The three *rampant* lions (on their hind legs) are from the Earl of Pembroke, after whom the College is named. The College's

royal patron, James I of England/James VI of Scotland is represented by the red *cinquefoil* (five-petal) rose for England and the green thistle for Scotland.

16th Century: Broadgates Hall Pembroke was originally a hostel for law students and is reputed to include the oldest surviving Oxford hall, Broadgates. The Principal of Broadgates, Randolph, served as ambassador for Elizabeth I in Scotland from 1559, where he became a friend of Mary, Queen of Scots until accused of supporting the rebellion of James Stuart. In

1568 he went to Russia to secure trading rights from Ivan IV "the Terrible", and succeeded.

17th Century: Earl of Pembroke An Abingdon merchant, Thomas Tesdale of Glympton, Oxfordshire, and a Berkshire clergyman, Richard Wightwick, put up the money to transform Broadgates Hall into Pembroke College. Their idea was to provide places at Oxford for boys from Abingdon School, modeled on Westminster College's channelling students to New College. In 1624 King James I signed the letters patent to create Pembroke College, named after William Herbert, the third Earl of Pembroke. The Earl was an alumnus of New College and was serving as Lord Chamberlain and Chancellor of the University; he had promoted the creation of the college.

17th Century: James I The thistle is appropriate to represent King James VI of Scotland (1566–1625), who became also James I of England. The flower associated with the Earl of Pembroke is a teasel, formally called the *Dipsacus* genus in the family *Caprifoliaceae,* looks like a thistle. James I is remembered by many for sponsoring the revered King James Version of the Bible. He was well educated and Protestant and helped Britain advance in the arts and sciences. He ruled Scotland as James VI from 1567 (one year old when crowned, he was represented by Regents until he came of age) till his death, and ruled England and Ireland as James I from 1603 until his death, the first monarch to rule over both England and Scotland. When Elizabeth I died without offspring in 1567, the English accepted a Scottish monarch because James, Elizabeth's nephew, was her closest relative, and he was Protestant. However, James fought often with England's Parliament and an uneasy peace prevailed. The Gunpowder Plot was a plan by some Catholics to blow up the Houses of Parliament. A member of the group, Guy Fawkes, was found in a basement with barrels of gunpowder, on 5 November 1605, while James was in the building. A nursery rhyme serves as a mnemonic:

"Remember, remember, / The fifth of November", which is also known as Bonfire Night. James I's son Charles I promoted his father's views on the divine right of kings, he caused a civil war and in 1649 was beheaded, England's only regicide.

Pembroke College entrance.

18th Century—Johnson Famed alumnus Samuel Johnson was too poor to pay Pembroke's bills (the College's nickname is "'Broke" and it has an exaggerated reputation for being poor and thereby costing students more), so he dropped out. He created the first modern dictionary. His entry under oats was: "A grain which in England is generally given to horses, but in Scotland supports the people." He was later awarded an honorary degree by the University. Two of his desks, and other possessions, are displayed in the college. He always spoke well of Pembroke, recalling the college's many poets: "We were a nest of singing birds."

19th Century—Smithson Alumnus James Smithson, whose generous 1846 bequest founded the Smithsonian Institution in

Washington, D.C. (despite his never having stepped foot in the United States) was an undergraduate at Pembroke, under the name "James Lewis Macie". After the death of his mother he changed his name to that of his natural father.

20th Century—The Shire J. R. R. Tolkien was a Fellow of Pembroke in 1925–1945. There he wrote *The Hobbit* and the first two volumes of *The Lord of the Rings.* Since 2013, Pembroke sponsors an annual Tolkien lecture on fantasy literature. A student website (thestudentroom. co.uk) says Pembroke is ". . . more the Shire than Mordor. The hall is imposing and the buildings are classic Oxford old, but it's not a scary place. The college is widely acknowledged as a friendly one." If you dare to leave safe Hobbit turf for Mordor, here are amusing directions: https://bit.ly/2LKQTjC.

20th Century—USA Several Pembroke alumni who were Rhodes Scholars became American statesmen, notably Senators J. William Fulbright, a Democrat who established the Fulbright Program, and Richard G. Lugar, a Republican; they chaired the Senate Foreign Relations Committee for 21 years between them (Lugar was also Ranking Member for six more years). Lugar won the Fulbright Award. Philip Lader served as US Ambassador to the UK in 1997–2001; John Kerr, Baron Kerr of Kinlochard, served as UK Ambassador to the USA in 1995–1997; so in 1997, both the US Ambassador in London and the UK Ambassador in Washington were Pembroke alumni.

Current Head of House The Master since 2013 is Dame Lynne Janie Brindley, DBE. She was the first-ever female Chief Executive of the British Library in 2000–2012. Following a first-class degree in music at the University of Reading, Brindley studied at the School of Librarianship, University College London, where she was awarded the Sir John MacAlister Medal as top student. She was librarian of the British Library of Political and Economic Science at the London School of Economics, and then became librarian and then Pro Vice-Chancellor of the University of Leeds. Brindley has worked to prevent libraries becoming "book museums". She says: "By the year 2020, 40 percent of UK research monographs will be available in electronic format only, while a further 50 percent will be produced in both print and digital. A mere 10 percent of new titles will be available in print alone by 2020."

Academic and Bumps Standing The College ranked 24th on the 2006–16 average and 13th in the 2016 Norrington Table. It jumped to third place in 2017, and fell back to 25th pace in 2018. Its state-school intake is about 50 percent. Pembroke is a powerhouse on the river. The Pembroke men's first eight was Head of the River in 1872, 1995, 2003, and 2013. In 2017 the men's first eight held its own in 4th place. The women's first eight bumped Wadham to become Head of the River, so the Pembroke women's first eight has led in 2000–2003, 2012, and now 2018. Pembroke won the "double headship trophy" in 2003. On points Pembroke has been in 1st place in both 2017 and 2018. Pembroke shares its boathouse with St Edmund's Hall. It is close to the river and fills as many as 12 shells in Summer Eights. Female undergraduates were first admitted to Pembroke in 1979; 40 years later, about half the students are female.

QUEEN'S COLLEGE, THE

Highlights

- The eagles are canting arms for founder Robert de Eglesfield.
- The college coat is differenced by a mullet on the first or lead eagle.
- Formally, the name of the college is The Queen's College.
- Created as a home in Oxford for young men from the north of England.

Arms, Blazon *Argent three Eagles displayed Gules beaked and legged Or on the breast of the first a Mullet of six points of the last.*

Arms, Origin Ancient. Predates the College of Arms, founded in 1484.

Arms, Meaning The three displayed eagles are from the canting arms (i.e., arms using a device to illustrate, or pun on, the name) of the founder. The added six-pointed mullet on the lead eagle, top left (*dexter*), is a mark of difference for the College. The mullet itself is a *mark of cadency,* differencing Robert as the third son of his father Robert de Eglesfield, but normally placed by itself and not on a device of the arms.

Founder The college was founded by Robert de Eglesfield of Eaglesfield, Cumberland. He was chaplain to Queen Philippa of Hainault, wife of Edward III, and he named the college in her honour, while putting his own arms on the college shield.

14th century—Robert de Eglesfield (c.1295–1349). Eglesfield's father's family held lands in and near Eaglesfield, near Cockermouth in Cumberland. At 21, Robert was a yeoman for Sir Anthony Lucy, Lord of Cockermouth. By 1331, he was carrying out minor royal administrative duties for the king. To provide him with income, he was put on the staff of the rectory of Brough, Westmorland in 1332, though not ordained a priest until the following year;

he did not permanently reside in his parish. He acquired some lands in Middlesex and was one of Queen Philippa's chaplains. To found The Queen's College, he traded the site for his manor of Renwick and added his own funds, in a year when he was serving as a Member of Parliament for Cumberland. He is listed as Provost in a deed dated 1347 and lived in the College in 1348. His remains were interred in the chapel, as he requested.In 1343, Philippa secured for the College a small hospital in Southampton that became a growing source of income.

15th century—Cumberland Connection
Mindful of the "poverty and lack of letters" of the men of Cumberland and Westmorland from which Eglesfield came, he asked for preference to be given to them and to his own relatives, to provide clergymen for the region. In addition, the college was to provide charity for the poor. The preference for inhabitants of Cumberland and Westmorland, starting after 1400, became a monopoly, making Queen's a colony of students from the British north-west.

17th century Queen's prospered in Elizabeth's reign, becoming one of the most popular Oxford colleges. It gradually embraced the tutorial system. Williamson donated a building in 1671–72, and the magnificent library was built in 1693–96 to house a new collection.

18th century By the 1730s, Queen's was the only Oxford college to be housed entirely in

Baroque buildings. The Front Quad, which has been called "the grandest piece of classical architecture in Oxford", was heavily influenced by the famed architect Nicholas Hawksmoor, who also produced some "extravagant" designs that were never executed. Queen's experienced the same decline during the century that afflicted most colleges in Oxford.

The Queen's College, Front Quad.

19th century In the early Victorian period, Queen's enjoyed the revival and reform that came to Oxford. Since the late nineteenth century it developed a strong academic reputation, while gifts and prudent management made it prosperous.

Today, candidates from all backgrounds are welcomed and northerners no longer have preference. However, the College respects its history, and values its ancient links with Cumberland, Westmorland, and Yorkshire.

Current Head of House The Provost since 2008 of Queen's is Paul Anthony Madden, FRS, FRSE. In 1984–2005 he was Fellow in Chemistry at Queen's and Senior Tutor of the college and Chairman of the University Information Technology Committee. In 2004–2008 he was Professor of Physical Chemistry and Director of Centre for Science at Extreme Conditions at the University of Edinburgh. He was awarded the Mulliken Medal of the University of Chicago for his achievements in Theoretical and Physical Chemistry. He was elected to the Fellowship of the Royal Society in 2001 and is also a Fellow of the Royal Society of Edinburgh.

Academic and Bumps Standing Queen's had a decline in its Norrington Table placement in 2006–2016, but bounced back in 2017. In 2018, Queen's ranked 19th on the Norrington Table. In 1833, Queen's was Head of the River, a one-off. In 2018 Summer Eights, the Queen's men's first eight kept its place on the river at 18th. The women's first eight fell one place from 35th to 36th. Since Queen's entered four crews, it had a better result on points, holding its place at #25.

REGENT'S PARK COLLEGE

Highlights

- From the beginning, has had Baptist ties.
- Named for the park in London where they once were.
- For a small college, high academic standing.
- Competes in Eights on the river.

Arms, Blazon *Argent on a Cross Gules an open Bible proper irradiated Or the pages inscribed with the words DOMINUS JESUS in letters sable on a chief wavy azure a fish Or.*

Arms, Origin Original Grant, 3 March 1958.

Arms, Meaning The cross of St George identifies the institution as English and probably Christian. The Bible and the fish (as symbol of Jesus, from the Greek word for fish ΙΧΘΥΣ, ICHTHUS—an acronym for the Greek for "Jesus Christ Son of God, Savior"—identify the institution as Christian and Bible-centered. The blue water line in chief references baptism. A clever shield because it succinctly expresses Baptist theology.

Arms, Full Achievement The full achievement of the arms includes a motto—*Omnia probate quod bonus tenet.* From St. Paul's First Epistle to the Thessalonians 5:21, it is translated: "Test all things; hold fast to that which is good." The full achievement also includes a crest resembling the facade of the building the college occupied in the Regent's Park area of London.

18th–19th centuries Regent's Park College originated as the Baptist Education Society in 1752. In 1810 it became the Stepney Academy, in East London. It helped Baptist students apply to Oxford University, and their number grew from three in 1827 to 26 in 1850. In 1856 the Academy moved across London to Regent's Park, and adopted the park's name. The College's mission broadened to include any nonmembers of the Church of England. It offered a university education in the Arts and Law and trained future Baptist clergy as well as classical scholars (like W. H. D. Rouse). In 1841, Regent's Park College was affiliated with the University of London.

20th century In 1927, the College moved to its third and current site in Oxford. In 1957 it became a Permanent Private Hall (PPH) of the University of Oxford.

Current Head of House The Principal is Robert Anthony Ellis, born in Cardiff and educated at Regent's Park College. He received his DPhil from Oxford in 1984. He is an ordained minister in the Baptist Union of Great Britain and has served congregations in Milton Keynes and Bristol. He serves on the Advisory Committee of the Vatican-sponsored programme "Sport at the Service of Humanity". He has been Moderator of the Baptist Union of Great Britain Ministry Executive.

Regent's Park College.

Academic and Rowing Standing Regent's Park College ranked second of the six Permanent Private Halls on the Norrington Table during the decade 2006–2016. It was 32nd out of 37 colleges and PPHs. In 2017 it ranked 24th out of 35 colleges and PPHs. In 2018, Regent's Park ranked 5th of the six PPHs. On the boating front, Regent's Park shares a boathouse with New College and it regularly competes in the Eights races. It currently owns two boats, "Regent's Shark" for the men's crew and the lighter-weight "Bond Girls" for the women's crew. In 2018 Summer Eights the Regent's Park men's eight ranked 52nd at the start and gained one bump to 51st place. The Regent's Park women's eight ranked 46h and bumped once and was bumped once, for a net of no change. Regent's Park was the only college/hall to net zero bumps in 2018, so it was *the median boat* for women.

SOMERVILLE COLLEGE

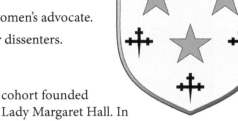

Highlights

- Named for famed Scottish mathematician and women's advocate.
- Founded by a committee that wanted a home for dissenters.
- Was famously used as a hospital in World War I.

Arms, Blazon *Argent three Mullets in chevron reversed Gules between six Crosses crosslet fitched Sable* (for Somerville).

Arms, Origin The College's arms are those of the Somerville family in Scotland, differenced by having one fewer cross crosslet fitchy (six instead of seven). The college is named after mathematician Mary Somerville, née Fairfax.

Arms, Meaning Mullets are supposed to be spurs in English heraldry, but one wonders how they can be spurs if they are shown in numbers greater than two. The French ending (-ville) of the Somerville name suggests that the Scottish Somervilles were of Norman ancestry. The shield has six crosslets fitchy, implying defense of the faith. The college uses the Somerville family's puzzling motto, *Donec rursus impleat orbem*, which can be translated "Until it/he/she fills the world again," probably meaning when Christ comes again.

19th century—Foundation In June 1878, the "Association for the Higher Education of Women" was formed, aiming for the eventual creation of a college for women in Oxford. The chief promoter of a woman's college was Edward Talbot, Warden of Keble College. Talbot favored a college for Anglican women. His

Mary Somerville.

cohort founded Lady Margaret Hall. In 1879, a second committee formed to create a college that would welcome dissenters. It included A. H. D. Acland, Thomas Hill Green, A. G. Vernon Harcourt, George William Kitchin, Henry Nettleship, John Percival, William Sidgwick, and Mary Ward. Their efforts led to the founding of Somerville Hall, named for Scottish mathematician and science writer Mary Somerville. She was admired by the founders both for her scholarship and her religious and political views. She advocated equal access of women to the vote and to education.

20th century—Temporary Hospital. During World War I Somerville was converted into a military hospital. Somerville students relocated to Oriel College. Notable patients who stayed in Somerville include poets Robert Graves and Siegfried Sassoon. *How unlike you to crib my idea of going to the Ladies' College at Oxford*, Sassoon wrote to Graves in 1917. At Somerville College, Graves met his first love, a nurse and professional pianist named Marjorie. He wrote: *I enjoyed my stay at Somerville. The sun shone, and the discipline was easy.* After the war, the move back by Somerville took time, creating problems and an incident in spring 1919 known as the "Oriel raid", in which male stu-dents made a hole in the wall dividing the sexes. In 1919 the Principal (Emily Penrose) and Fellows returned to Somerville. Alumna Vera Brittain wrote about the impact of the war in Oxford and paid tribute to the work of the Principal, Miss Penrose, in her memoir *Testament of Youth*.

20th century—Alumnae Among the famous alumnae of Somerville are Margaret Thatcher, Indira Gandhi, Dorothy Hodgkin, Cornelia Sorabji, Vera Brittain, and Dorothy L. Sayers.

Current Head of House The Principal since 2017 is Baroness Royall of Blaisdon, Jan Royall. She was appointed to the House of Lords in 2004 as a Life Peer and in 2005 became a Government Spokesperson for Health, International Development, Foreign and Commonwealth Affairs. She became Chief Whip in the Lords and member of the Privy Council and in 2008 became Leader of the Lords and a member of the cabinet. Prior to 2004, she was a senior adviser in the European Commission before heading its office in Wales. Following a degree in Spanish and French at the University of London, her first job was importing flowers into Europe from Colombia. For six years she was General Secretary of the British Labour Group in the European Parliament and then worked for the Leader of the Opposition, Neil Kinnock. In 2010–15, Baroness Royall was Leader of the Opposition in the Lords and continues as an active back-bencher.

Academic and Rowing Standing When it was a woman-only college, Somerville ranked near to top on the Norrington Table. After the men moved in, Somerville's ranking fell to 25th on the Norrington Table based on the average score for 2006–2016, but rose to 16th in 2016, and settling back to 22nd in 2017 and 2018. Having devoted most of its life to educating the New Woman, the college views its new challenge as educating the New Man. On the river, Somerville was a powerhouse in 1980–1993, with the most Headships (eight) in Eights Week of any other women's crews. However, Pembroke took their place since 2000, with six Headships for their women's crews. In 2018, Somerville's first men's eight started in 32nd place and was bumped once to 33rd. The first women's eight continues to do better, starting in 12th place and ending in 13th. On overall points, Somerville stayed in 31st place.

ST ANNE'S COLLEGE

Highlights

- Named for the mother of Mary by Principal Eleanor Plumer.
- The coat of arms is that of Viscount Plumer, Eleanor's father.
- Created for unhoused students, it still seeks the challenged.

Arms, Blazon *Gules on a Chevron between in chief two Lion's heads erased Argent and in base a Sword of the second pommel and hilt Or and enfiled with a wreath of Laurel proper three Ravens Sable* (for Plumer).

Arms, Origin Assumed, 1952. St Anne's was originally called the Society for Home Students, a place for students without a college affiliation. The fourth Principal of the Society, Eleanor Plumer, received a large gift pledge from Amy Hartland in 1942, and named the Society for St Anne (the Virgin Mary's mother by Christian and Islamic tradition). Hartland left her entire large estate to the college in 1945. In 1952 St Anne's became a full college. Plumer allowed the use of the arms of her father, Field Marshal Herbert Viscount Plumer, credited with a major victory at Ypres. Plumer was one of the few military leaders whose reputation was enhanced during World War I.

Arms, Meaning Two lions may signify England. The sword and laurel wreath would reference Plumer's military rank and victory. The birds are probably a canting reference to the word plume.

19th century—A Place for Women in Lodgings The creation of Lady Margaret Hall and Somerville College were important steps in opening an Oxford education to women. The Society of Home-Students, the forerunner of St Anne's College, allowed young women to live less expensively in lodgings across the city, and to attend lectures and tutorials.

20th century—From Society to College The original idea behind the Society—opening to more young people the opportunities offered by Oxford University—has endured beyond the transition to full collegiate life. In 1942, the Society of Home-Students became the St Anne's Society, and in turn a full College of the University, complete with Royal Charter, in 1952.

21st century—A New Mission. With full integration of men and women into the College's life, the new mission is to connect the ideals of the University with those who have not previously had the chance to encounter them. First it was any women, then poor women, and now it is anyone for whom an Oxford education is a challenge because of finances or cultural background. Once known as strong in the Humanities, St Anne's now covers the full range of academic disciplines: in the Social Sciences, the Life and Medical Sciences, and the Mathematical and Physical Sciences. St Anne's is one of the few colleges in Oxford able to offer affordable rooms to almost all 430 undergraduate students.

Head of House The Principal of St Anne's since 2017 is Helen Mary King, QPM a retired police officer, whose service included the Cheshire Constabulary and the Metropolitan Police Service, where she reached the rank of Assistant Commissioner. Born in Bishop's Stortford, Hertfordshire, King is the daughter of a senior civil servant and was educated first at an all-girls comprehensive school and then at the Perse School for Girls in Cambridge. In 1983, she matriculated at St Anne's to study Philosophy, Politics and Economics (PPE), graduating in 1986 with a BA degree. In 1994, she completed a Master of Arts degree at the University of Manchester and in 2003, she completed a postgraduate diploma at the University of Cambridge. In 2014, King joined the Metropolitan Police Service as assistant commissioner for territorial policing, overseeing policing in London's 32 Boroughs. In 2016, she was appointed assistant commissioner in charge of training and professional standards. She is the first police officer to head an Oxbridge college. In the 2011 New Year Honours, King was awarded the Queen's Police Medal (QPM) in recognition of her service as an Assistant Chief Constable of Merseyside Police.

St Anne's College boathouse, shared.

Academic and Rowing Standing On the Norrington Table, St Anne's ranked 17th on the 2006–16 average, 28th in 2016, 19th in 2017, and 24th in 2018. St Anne's shares a boathouse with St Hugh's and Wadham. The St Anne's men's first eight started at 27th in the 2018 Summer Eights and was bumped three times. The women's first eight started at 15th and was bumped once. On points, St Anne's ranked 23rd at the beginning of the week and fell to 27th by the end.

ST ANTONY'S COLLEGE

Highlights

- The College is named for three different Antonys.
- A statue is erected to the wife of Sir Antonin Besse, the founder.
- Another is erected to St Anthony of Padua.
- But St Anthony the Great of Alexandria is the official nominee.

Arms, Blazon *Or on a Chevron between three Tau Crosses Gules as many pierced Mullets of the field.*

Arms, Origin Original Grant, 30 November 1953.

Arms, Meaning The tinctures on the arms are for Egypt's desert—gold (*or*) for the sand, and red (*gules*) for the the Red Sea. The mullets echo the trademark of the founder's firm. The T crosses are Franciscan taus.

Arms, Three Nominees The arms reference *three* Antonys—Antonin Besse, St Anthony of Padua, and St Anthony the Great of Alexandria (the apostrophe in the name of the college might appropriately go *after* the final "s" in St Antony's):

1 Sir Antonin Besse Sir Antonin was a French merchant who founded the college in 1950 by donating the required funds. The mullets on the chevron on the college's shield invoke the trademark of Besse's company in Aden (https://bit.ly/2muBl8C).

2 St Anthony of Padua was a Franciscan friar, follower of St Francis and Patron Saint of the Poor. The three crosses on the arms are the "Franciscan taus", worn by Franciscans. By not having a top arm, the crosses are considered the most humble. The tau is also considered a sign of forgiveness and protection. The only college statue to an Anthony is the one to St Anthony of Padua in the Hilda Besse Building.

3 St Anthony the Great of Egypt, born about 254 A.D., by legend the first Christian monk and the first abbot, whose biography was written by St Athanasius, archbishop of Alexandria. For the first decade after the college was founded, it was presumed that the primary sainted nominee was St Anthony of Padua. However, the college decided in 1961 that St Anthony the Great of Egypt should be the primary nominee, partly because of the College's strong focus on studies of the Middle East

21st century St Antony's worldly dons are often relied on to respond to media inquiries about current news. Sometimes, as in 2018 when the Oxford Union invited a right-wing German to speak, St Antony's provided commentators for both sides of the issue.

Statue of St Anthony of Padua.

Current Head of House The Warden since 2017 is Professor Roger Goodman, who came to the College in 1982 to start his doctoral work in social anthropology. After stints as a

Junior Research Fellow at St Antony's and a year at Imperial College London, he became a Reader in the Department of Sociology at the University of Essex in 1989–1993. He returned to Oxford to become the first Lecturer in the Social Anthropology of Japan and a Fellow of St Antony's. He succeeded to the Nissan Professorship of Modern Japanese Studies in 2003. In 2004, he was appointed as the inaugural Head of the new School of Interdisciplinary Area Studies (SIAS). In 2008–2017, he was Head of Oxford's Social Sciences Division. He is a Fellow of the UK Academy of Social Sciences and has chaired the Academy's Council since 2015. His research is mainly on Japanese education and social policy, having published two monographs with Oxford University Press, *Japan's International Youth* (1990) and *Children of the Japanese State* (2000).

Academic and Rowing Standing St Antony's is not ranked academically because it does not admit undergraduates. Students at the College are engaged primarily in graduate teaching programs and secondarily in graduate research. It did fill four boats in 2018 to compete in Summer Eights, two men's and two women's. The first men's eight started in 31st place and was bumped once. The first women's eight started in 28th place and held its own. On points, St Antony's started and ended in 30th place.

ST BENET'S HALL

Highlights

- Ampleforth College founded St Benet's in 1897.
- The St Benet's arms were adopted hatless from Ampleforth.
- Westminster Abbey was once the Benedictine Abbey of St Peter.

Arms, Blazon and Origin *Per fesse dancetté Or and Azure a chief per pale Gules and of the second charged on the dexter with two Keys in saltire Or and Argent and on the sinister with a Cross Flory between five Martlets of the first.*

Arms, Origin Adopted. Originally granted to Ampleforth Abbey, 1922. The Hall does not use the abbot's hat (the *galero,* with three rows of tassels).

Arms, Meaning The nominee of the hall is St Benet, i.e., St Benedict of Nursia. Born AD 480 in today's Norcia, near Perugia in Umbria, Italy, Benedict founded the first Christian monastic order. He died in 547 in Monte Cassino and is the patron saint of students and of Europe. The arms reference St Peter through the keys at top left (*dexter*); Westminster Abbey is dedicated to him. At top right (*sinister*) the gold cross flory and the five martlets reference St Edward the Confessor, the last significant Anglo-Saxon king and the chief patron and founder of Westminster Abbey, where all England's monarchs have been crowned since 1066. The lower two-thirds of the shield signifies the Benedictine abbots of Westminster. The fields of gold (*or*) and blue (*azure*), representing sun and the water of the Thames, are divided by a zigzag line (*dancetté*). The last Benedictine abbot of Westminster was the wise and gentle John Feckenham (c 1515–1584), an Oxford Doctor of Divinity; his abbey was suppressed by Elizabeth I in 1560.

10th–13th centuries A Benedictine Abbey was created on the Thames c965. King (Saint) Edward the Confessor rebuilt St Peter's

Church, c1042–60, with the intent of making it the site of coronations of future monarchs. Henry III rebuilt the church again in 1245 as St Peter's Abbey.

16th–17th centuries Henry VIII dissolved the English Benedictine monasteries in the 1530s, but he gave Westminster Abbey the status of a cathedral. When St Paul's was built, it was called East Minster and St Peter's became Westminster. (Some stones and revenue from Westminster were used to build St Paul's—"robbing Peter to pay Paul".) By 1607 only one of the Westminster monks was left alive—Fr Sigebert Buckley. He professed a group of English monks in prison before he died, passing on to them the rights of the English Benedictine Congregation. In 1615, the monks went to France and re-established themselves in an abandoned church of St Lawrence near Nancy, keeping alive the English Benedictine order.

18th–20th centuries After the French Revolution, the monks were expelled from France and moved back to England. They were given property in Ampleforth, Yorkshire by Lady Anne Fairfax of Gilling Castle. In 1803, the monastery school opened. In 1897, St Benet's Hall was founded for monks to live while reading for Oxford degrees. By 1900, Ampleforth Abbey was a community of nearly 100 monks. The first Abbot died in office in 1924, succeeded by Fr Edmund Matthews, who appointed Fr Paul Nevill as the college's Headmaster. These two men together made the college's reputation. At its height in the mid-1960s the Abbey had 169 monks; the number has since fallen to about 60. The 8th Abbot of Ampleforth, Fr Cuthbert Madden, was elected in 2005. St. Benet's Hall is administered by a Trust chaired by the abbot. It is a wholly owned subsidiary of Ampleforth Abbey.

21st century Until 2016, St Benet's Hall admitted only male undergraduates. In autumn 2016, the author and his wife, Alice Tepper Marlin, attended the first co-ed brunch at St Benet's, which was the last of the Oxford colleges and halls to become coeducational.

St Benet's arms etched in stone.

Current Head of House The Master of St Benet's is Professor Werner Jeanrond, who notes: "In the twelfth century, students at Oxford gathered around a Master to grow in knowledge and wisdom. Nine hundred years later, St Benet's Hall is an echo, perhaps the closest there is, of that way of life."

Academic and Bumps Standing The Norrington Table ranked St Benet's 34th (out of 37) on the average 2006–2016, and 34th again in 2017. In 2018, St Benet's ranked 3rd in the Norrington Table among the six PPHs. As a tiny hall, St Benet's gets great credit for entering the boat races, with both men's and women's eights. The St Benet's men's eight started 2018 Eights Week in the 55th position (out of 92 boats) and held its own during the four days of racing. The new women's eight started in 73rd place and suffered five bumps, to end in 78th place out of 79 boats.

ST CATHERINE'S COLLEGE

Highlights

- Originally a club for unhoused students, now dubbed St Catz.
- The students wanted to row. The boat club led to a college.
- Danish architect opted for a bell tower . . . but no chapel to put it on.
- In 2018 St Catz came in 3rd on the Norrington Table.

Arms, Blazon *Sable a Saltire Ermine between four Catherine Wheels Or.*

Arms, Origin The arms, according to officials of St Catz (as it is usually called), were granted by the College of Arms in 1964, two years after the College opened. The Letter Patent, usually signed and sealed by all the three Kings of Arms on behalf of the College of Arms, is reportedly in a secure location at St Catz. A printed source confirms the granting of arms for St Catz, with the date of the grant June 10, 1963, which could mean that there was a delay of at least six months from the commitment to the preparation and signing of the Letter Patent.

Arms, Full Achievement Below the shield is a motto: *Nova et Vetera*—"The new and the old." The grant of arms normally shows the full achievement, with a crest and a mantle.

Arms, Meaning The name of the college and the "Catherine wheels" in the four fields created by the ermine saltire refer to St Catherine of Alexandria, Egypt, then a great center of learning. A saltire is associated with martyrdom. St Catherine's badge is a wheel. St Hugh's also has a *sable* field with a *saltire ermine,* but where St Catz has a *Catherine wheel or,* St Hugh's has a *fleur-de-lys or.*

Nominee—St Catherine A virgin martyr, St Catherine was the daughter of non-believing parents but became a Christian at 18. She is one of the two saints that St Joan of Arc, a

millennium later, said talked with her. Roman Emperor Maxentius (ruled 306–312) wanted her to marry one of his sons if she would give up her Christian beliefs. He brought her to Rome, but she continued to inveigh publicly against worshipping idols. Confronted by 50 philosophers, she refuted them and they were burned alive for being unable to rebut her arguments. She refused to deny her faith and marry the emperor's son. Incensed, Maxentius had her imprisoned and beaten for two hours. Continuing to refuse Maxentius' proposals, she was sentenced to be broken on a spiked wheel, but it fell to pieces at her touch. Maxentius had her beheaded instead. Maxentius was defeated by Constantine in 312. Catherine is today a revered Catholic and Eastern Orthodox saint, whose feast day is November 25. Some crusty historians doubt she existed, suggesting that her legend was created centuries later. She is nonetheless embraced as their patron saint by female students, young women in the workplace, nuns, philosophers, preachers and, naturally, wheelwrights.

19th century—Social Club The College was originally formed as the Delegacy of Non-Collegiate Students, founded in 1868 to offer a university education without the costs of college membership. The social role of a college was created by the Delegacy's students, who met in a meeting room in a hall on Catte Street under the unofficial name of St Catherine's Club. The Club was officially recognized by the University in 1931 as St Catherine's Society.

20th century–Emergence of the College In 1956 the University Delegates offered the Society a path to college status. By 1960 Sir Alan Bullock matched some University funding with £1 million from Sir Alan Wilson and Sir Hugh Beaver. With £2.5 million funded, the college opened in 1962, while still under construction. It was the year that I came up to Oxford and I remember the tentative nature of the opening. By 1974 St Catz was in full operation and was one of the first five men's colleges to admit women as full members, the other four being Brasenose, Hertford, Jesus, and Wadham. St Catz staked out and purchased from Merton College eight acres on part of Holywell Great Meadow, on the eastern side of Oxford looking over the Cherwell. Its glass-and-concrete buildings by the Danish architect Arne Jacobsen. The buildings combined modern construction materials with the traditional quadrangle layout, and the architect followed through on his design to the furniture, lampshades and cutlery. The dining hall is distinctive for its slate floor and its 350 seats, the largest capacity of any Oxford college. Jacobsen's plans for the college did not include a chapel; the college's annual Christmas carol concert is held in the chapel of Harris Manchester College. The College does have a prominent bell tower. It also has lecture theatres and seminar rooms, spacious common rooms, a music house, two student computer rooms, a small gym, squash courts and a punt house on the Cherwell.

Current Head of House The Master since 2002 is Roger Ainsworth, who was educated at Lancaster Royal Grammar School, was apprenticed at Rolls-Royce Aeroengines, studied at Jesus College, Oxford and was awarded a First Class BA in 1973, and became Doctor of Philosophy in 1976. Dr. Ainsworth then worked in industry, initially for Rolls-Royce and later for the Atomic Energy Research Establishment. He returned to Oxford in 1985 as a tutorial Fellow of St Catherine's College. He became Professor of Engineering Science in 1998. He was elected Master of St Catherine's in 2002. He is also a Pro-Vice-Chancellor of the University. In academic year 1999 he served as Senior Proctor. He has also been Chair of the Board of the Department for Continuing Education. Ainsworth is a Visiting Professor at the École Polytechnique Fédérale de Lausanne, a member of the Engineering and Physical Sciences Research Council, a member of the British Association for the Advancement of Science and a member of the Oxford Philomusica Advisory Council. He is Chairman of the Hinksey Fields Protection Group, Chairman of the Broad Street Plan Group of the Oxford Preservation Trust, trustee of the Oxford School of Drama and a Fellow of the Royal Aeronautical Society. He was appointed a Knight of the Order of the Dannebrog by HM The Queen of Denmark in recognition of his promotion of the work of Arne Jacobsen, the Danish architect who designed St Catherine's.

St Catz with bell tower showing from behind.

Academic and Bumps Standing The Norrington Table ranks St Catz 16th on the 2006–2016 average, 10th in 2016, 24th in 2017, and 3rd in 2018, a major improvement. The Catz boats are housed in the Long Bridges Boat House. The blades of the college oars are distinctively decorated with Catherine Wheels. Boat Club historian Don Barton reports that six years after the University established a society for non-collegiate students in 1868, members founded St Catharine's Club, using the Cambridge spelling. The following year, the Boat Club was created, and the spelling was corrected to St Catherine's in 1919. Soon after, the society took its name from that of the Boat Club. The Boat Club thus gave the name to both the original society and the College that it grew into. The Boat Club first took part in Torpids and Summer Eights in 1876, and produced the first crew to make seven bumps in the then six days (now four) of Summer Eights. Three crews made six bumps in Eights in 1949. The Women's 1st Eight won Head of

the River in Torpids in 2007. Skipping ahead to 2018, the St Catz men's first eight bumped on the first day but was bumped on the third and fourth days, for a net minus of one bump. The women's first eight got its bump on the fourth day. Bottom line, on points, St Catz rose from 14th to 13th place on the river. With a net of eight bumps for the six St Catz crews (four men's, two women's), St Catz ranked 5th, tied with Green Templeton and New College.

ST CROSS COLLEGE

Highlights

- The College was created to accommodate graduates.
- It has a grant for its coat of arms.
- Students early on wanted to compete with other colleges.
- St Cross students row in Wolfson's seven boats.

Arms, Blazon *Argent a Cross potent Purpure a quarter counterchanged.*

Arms, Origin Original Grant 2 November 2000. Thanks to the following three people who contacted me after *Oxford Today* published my article on the heraldry of the Oxford colleges to note that the St Cross arms are granted: Anthony Weale, former Secretary of Faculties and Academic Registrar, Oxford University; Ella Bedrock, in the communications office, St Cross College; and Sir Mark Jones, Master of St Cross College.

Arms, Meaning The motto is in the full achievement of the coat of arms, *Ad Quattuor Cardines Mundi* ("To the four corners of the world") but not in the blazon on the grant. The *Cross Potent* is one of many variations of the Christian cross in heraldic use that emerged at the time of the First Crusade (1095–1099). It was one of the crosses used on their shields by the Teutonic Knights. It would surely have been seen in England as a Christian religious

symbol at the time it was created, although pre-Christian examples of the use of the T-tipped cross have been found.

Arms, Nominee The College was named, say official sources, after St Cross Road, which links South Parks Road to the north and Longwall Street to the south, where it also meets Holywell Street (formerly Holywell Lane). The road runs by the ancient Holy Cross Church, which gave the road its name. The original buildings of St Cross College were located on the grounds of the church. The arms represent the name of the road. The St Cross Latin Grace rejoices in honour of the Holy Cross.

Foundation (1965) St Cross was founded by the University as a graduate college, at the same time as Wolfson and for the same reason. (Kellogg College was founded by the University later for a different purpose, i.e., continuing education.) St Cross College is entirely secular; it has no chaplain. A new college was needed to provide a college affiliation for a large number of new postwar fellows and graduate students, responding to the increased number of subjects taught at the University in the sciences and new fields such as archaeology and social sciences. The teachers were entitled to a college assignment, with the meals, lodging, stipends, and the sense of belonging that come with it—including functioning under a cozier coat of arms than the University-wide *Dominus Illuminatio Mea*. The University was getting pushback, as existing colleges reached the limit of the number of fellows and graduate students after World War II they could absorb. Postwar policy in the United States was to finance the higher education of returning veterans. In Britain, Clement Attlee went beyond that, broadly expanding access to health care and education. Students at the church-affiliated PPHs were eager to be able to compete in more intercollegiate sports, as they continue to do. The University encouraged the expansion of some of the PPHs and moved a few of them toward college status, a concern being that the PPH give up links to a religious entity. Then the University decided to take the bull by the horns and in 1965 created a brand new residential college for graduates, i.e., St Cross. When St Cross was created, its graduate students wanted to compete in intercollegiate sports like any other college.

Buildings The college was originally provided with buildings on the site of the ancient Holy Cross Church, which has since been converted to a document-storage site for historic collections owned by Balliol College. From this site the College moved to one on the west side of St Giles among many PPHs and unaffiliated religious institutions such as the Quaker center. The ground under it is owned by the Anglo-Catholic Pusey House, named after Edward Bouverie Pusey, the man who led the Oxford Movement after John Henry Newman decamped to become a Roman Catholic. The proximity of Pusey House creates advantages for St Cross students. St Cross students may use facilities such as the Pusey House Library and Chapel.

St Cross Church, which gives its name to St Cross Road and thereby to the College.

Intellectual History The college's sharing of facilities with Pusey House means it shares somewhat in the rich intellectual and religious history of Pusey House. However, its main intellectual focus since World War II is in the sciences and it makes clear that it is formally unaffiliated with any religion.

Current Head of House The Master of St Cross since 2016 is Carole Souter CBE, FSA. She is former Chief Executive of the National Heritage Memorial Fund and Heritage Lottery Fund. Souter has degrees in Philosophy, Politics and Economics (BA, Oxon) and Victorian Studies (MA, University of London). By 2016, her career of more than 30 years included policy development and operational management in the public sector. She worked in the Department of Health, the Department of Social Security and the Cabinet Office. Souter joined the National Heritage Memorial Fund and Heritage Lottery Fund in 2003, having previously been Director of Planning and Development at English Heritage. She is also a lay canon of Salisbury Cathedral. In March 2016, Souter was appointed a trustee of Historic Royal Palaces. Souter was made a Commander of the Order of the British Empire (CBE) in 2011 for services to conservation. In

2014, she was elected a Fellow of the Society of Antiquaries of London. Souter is a Fellow of the Royal Society of Arts (FRSA). She was made an Honorary Fellow of Jesus College, Oxford in 2011.

Academic and Rowing Standing Since St Cross is only for graduate students, it is not included in the Norrington Table. It competes in the eights races by joining with the Wolfson boats. Wolfson filled seven shells in the 2018 Summer Eights. Wolfson came in *first* out of 34 colleges on the net average number of bumps per crew, with a total of 13. It moved up in the Head of the River standings from 4th to 3rd place. The first men's eight ended 5th and the first women's eight ended 6th.

ST EDMUND HALL

Highlights

- Keeps the title of hall (as does LMH), although it is now a college
- The oldest continuously operating hall in Oxford, dating to 1236
- Arms attributed to St Edmund of Abingdon
- But they are not his arms as Archbishop of Canterbury

Arms, Blazon *Or a Cross patonce Gules cantoned by four Cornish Choughs proper (for St Edmund of Abingdon).*

Arms, Origin Attributed arms of St Edmund of Abingdon. The four birds are also variously referred to as sea-pies and oyster-catchers. The choughs should not have the white wings shown in Brooke-Little's 1951 review of the Oxford coats of arms, a rare mistake for Brooke-Little.There is no record of the arms having been granted, but they are authoritative because they are ancient. They were "discovered" as the arms of St Edmund of Abingdon by a Benedictine monk-detective, Dom Wilfred Wallace, but Dom Wilfred concludes that the main devices used for the arms of Edmund when he became Archbishop of Canterbury were three suns, not choughs.

Arms, Meaning The black birds are called Cornish choughs, which were used by St Edmund of Abingdon (surnamed Rich by townspeople), the first Oxford MA to become Archbishop of Canterbury. The coat of arms is attributed to the Founder of the Hall, (St) Edmund Rich of Abingdon, a few miles south of Oxford. He was Archbishop of Canterbury 1210–1233. Below the college arms is found the Latin chronogram-dedication *Sanctus edmundus huius aulae lux* ("St Edmund, light of this Hall"). The text is rendered as sanCtVs edMVndVs hVIVs aVLae LVX. Adding the numerals (the capital letters) gives 1246, the date St Edmund was canonized.

13th century—Founding St Edmund is considered to have founded the hall in 1236, not long after the Dominicans established Blackfriars in 1221. It is the only surviving medieval Aularian ("Hall") house, giving the name of "Aularians" to SEH members. Its nominee was the first of many Oxonians to become Archbishop of Canterbury. The name St Edmund Hall (*Aula Sancti Edmundi*) first appears in a 1317 rental agreement. But early in the thirteenth century the site of the front quadrangle was owned by John de Bermingham, rector of Iffley, whose relatives in 1262 sold part of it to Thomas of Malmesbury, perpetual vicar of Cowley. In 1272 Thomas granted his part of the site to Oseney Abbey, which owned it until it was dissolved in 1539. The college library is in the deconsecrated 12th-century church of St Peter-in-the-East, including a crypt that is still consecrated. An SEH garden includes a seated bronze figure representing Edmund as an impoverished student, as most scholars in the earliest centuries were impecunious and lived in squalid conditions.

14th–17th centuries—Intellectual Independence The College has a long history of being independent of both Church and State. During the late 14th and early 15th centuries it was a bastion of John Wycliffe's supporters; college principal William Taylor was ultimately burned at the stake, and principal Peter Payne fled the country. In the late 17th century, the College incurred the Crown's anger for encouraging its members to remain loyal to the Scottish House of Stuart and to refuse to take the oath to the German House of Hanover (i.e., they were "non-jurors" or "not swearers"). Two such non-jurors were called out to the SEH Principal, who refused to act. But when brought before the University, they and four others were expelled. Boswell in his *Life of Dr Johnson* expressed sympathy for the six expelled students:

> "I talked of the recent expulsion of six students from the University of Oxford, who were Methodists, and would not desist from publicly praying and exhorting.

> JOHNSON. "Sir, that expulsion was extremely just and proper. What have they to do at University, who are not willing to be taught, but will presume to teach? Where is religion to be learnt, but at an University? Sir, they were examined, and found to be mighty arrogant fellows."

> BOSWELL. "But was it not hard, Sir, to expel them, for I am told they were good beings?"

> JOHNSON. "I believe they might be good beings; but they were not fit to be in the University of Oxford. A cow is a very good animal to be in a field; but we turn her out of the garden."

17th century—Early Buildings St Edmund Hall is on the north side of High Street ("the High"). The front quadrangle—in the middle of which is a medieval well—is bordered by the porters' lodge, the Old Dining Hall (1659), the college bar and buttery (with a mid-15th-century fireplace), a chapel, and an Old (late 17th century) Library above. The quadrangle includes some accommodations for students and fellows. (Modern accommodation and a dining hall are to the east of the quadrangle.)

20th century—Becomes a College St Edmund's Hall, also known as Teddy Hall or SEH, was made a college in 1957.

Current Head of House The Principal since 2009 is Professor Keith Gull CBE, FRS. He is a Wellcome Trust Principal Research Fellow and Professor of Molecular microbiology at the Sir William Dunn School of Pathology at Oxford. Gull was educated at Eston Grammar School and King's College London where he was awarded a first class Bachelor of Science degree in 1969 followed by a PhD in 1973. He then lectured at the University of Kent and held a personal chair. He moved to the University of Manchester where he spent the 1990s involved with the development of the School of Biological Sciences as Head of Biochemistry and Research Dean. He came to Oxford in 2002. He was Chairman of the Biochemical Society (1999–2002), and is a trustee of Cancer Research UK. His research has focused on how parasites cause disease, with his most cited peer-reviewed scientific papers being on different forms of *Trypanosoma* with more recent research being on the Leishmania parasite. After ten years as Principal Professor of St Edmund Hall, Gull will retire in 2018 academic year, to be succeeded by Kathy Willis. Keith Gull was awarded the Marjory Stephenson Prize from the Society for General Microbiology (1996), was elected Fellow of the Academy of Medical Sciences in 1999 and Fellow of the Royal Society (FRS) in 2003, and was awarded the CBE in 2004 for services to microbiology.

St Edmund Hall boathouse.

Academic and Bumps Standing The Norrington Table ranks Teddy Hall as 23rd on the 2006–2016 average, 21st in 2016, 23rd in 2017, and 29th in 2018. On the river (and even more on the rugby field, where SEH has dominated for decades), Teddy Hall has done a lot better. In the 2018 Summer Eights, the first men's eight got two bumps to end up in 9th place and the women's eight was bumped by New College but still ended in 8th place. Overall, on points, Teddy Hall rose from 9th to 8th place. Its 11 net bumps from five crews placed it second after Wolfson.

ST HILDA'S COLLEGE

Highlights

- Founded by Dorothea Beale, educator and suffragist.
- The unicorns and estoiles are from her family.
- Named after famed Abbess of Whitby Abbey.
- The petrified snake refers to a miracle of St Hilda.

Arms, Blazon *Azure on a Fesse Or between in chief two Unicorn's heads couped and in base a coiled Serpent Argent three Estoiles Gules.*

Arms, Origin Granted 1960, exact date not given.

Arms, Meaning. When the College was incorporated in 1926 it could not afford to pay the College of Arms for a grant of arms, so a seal was designed by Edmund New, with a bookplate, note paper and blazer badge based upon it. The first symbol of St Hilda's Hall was the ammonite fossil, consisting of whorled chambered shells, which was supposed to be coiled snakes petrified. This is now shown in the lower third of the St Hilda's College arms. The early seventeenth century *Lives of Women Saints of our Contrie of England* explains the association of snakes with St Hilda:

> In that monastery of Whitby, there was such an abundance of serpents, in the thick bushes and wilderness of the woods, that the virgins durst

not peep out of their Cells, or go to draw water. But by her prayers she obtained of God, that they might be turned into stones, yet so as the shape of serpents still remained. Which to this day, the stones of that place do declare, as eye-witnesses have testified.

The use of the ammonite with the motto *non frustra vixi* or "I lived not in vain" continued throughout St Hilda's history. It was the emblem of the College until the coat of arms was granted in 1960. The motto was not included in the grant of arms, although it is occasionally used. The top two-thirds of the coat of arms commemorates Dorothea Beale with its use of estoiles (stars with wavy limbs) and unicorns. Although no evidence could be found that the family was armigerous, all Beale families seem to have used a coat of arms with estoiles and a unicorn's head for their crest.

Founder—Dorothea Beale LL.D. (1831–1906) was born at 41 Bishopsgate Street, London, the fourth child and third daughter of Miles Beale, a surgeon, and his wife, Dorothea Margaret Complin, of Huguenot extraction. At 13, Dorothea attended lectures at Gresham College and at the Crosby Hall Literary Institution, and developed an aptitude for mathematics. Dorothea and her sisters went to the newly opened Queen's College, Harley Street. In 1849, Miss Beale was appointed mathematical tutor at Queen's College, and in 1854 she became head teacher in the school attached to the college. In 1858 Miss Beale was chosen out of fifty candidates to be principal of the Ladies' College, Cheltenham, the earliest proprietary girls' school in England, where she spent the rest of her career. When she began as principal, the school had 69 pupils and was struggling. The school grew to 500 pupils by 1880, and to more than 1,000 by 1912. The first residential training college for secondary women teachers, called St. Hilda's College, was sited in Cheltenham, opening in 1885. To give teachers-in-training the benefit of a year at Oxford, Miss Beale purchased in 1892 Cowley House, Oxford, and enabled the founding of St. Hilda's Hall for women in 1893. In 1901 it was incorporated with the Cheltenham training college as "St. Hilda's Incorporated College". Miss Beale identified herself with the movement for women's suffrage, being a vice-president of the central society. Signs of cancer became apparent in 1900. In 1901, the honorary freedom of the Borough of Cheltenham was awarded to her, for her work with the ladies' college. In 1902 the university of Edinburgh awarded her the honorary degree of LL.D., in recognition of her services to education, only the second woman to receive this honour. She died after a cancer operation. Her body was cremated and her ashes are buried in a small vault on the south side of the Lady chapel of Gloucester Cathedral.

Nominee—St Hilda She was born in Whitby, Yorkshire in 614 and became one of the foremost abbesses of Anglo-Saxon England. With Bishops Sts Colman of Lindisfarne and Cedd of the East Saxons, she led the Celtic party at the Synod of Whitby (663/664). She became abbess of Hartlepool Abbey, Durham, and in 654/655 was entrusted with the upbringing of King Oswiu's daughter, St Aelfflaed. The King gave Hilda the land on which she founded a double monastery of monks and nuns at Streaneshalch (now Whitby). Her abbey became one of the great religious centres of north-eastern England. Among its members was Caedmon, the earliest English Christian poet. In 663/664 Streaneshalch housed the Synod of Whitby, summoned to settle the dispute over whether the date of Easter should be Celtic or Roman. Like Colman, Hilda opposed the Roman party led by Northumbrian Bishop St. Wilfrid. Unlike Colman, Hilda submitted to Oswiu's decision in favour of Rome. She died in 680. Her feast day is November 17.

History St Hilda's was the last of the five women's colleges to be created, although St Anne's did not become a full college until 1952. Today, the College remains true to its roots and strives for equality as well as excellence. St Hilda's College reached its 125th anniversary in 2018, and its 10th anniversary as a coeducational college. In 2009, following the precedent set in 1979 by St Anne's College, the overwhelming majority of the College's alumnae decided to continue using the feminine plural, to honour the College's history and to take into account the fact that it will be many decades before its Senior Members are equally split between men and women. This custom is intended to reflect the College's origins as a female-only institution and does not seek to marginalise its male alumni. So St Hilda's has a Development and Alumnae Relations Office, even though many of its Alumnae are Alumni.

Current Head of House The Principal of St Hilda's since 2014 is Sir Gordon William Duff, FRCP, FMedSci, FRSE. He was the first male head of the formerly all-female college. He was previously Lord Florey Professor of Molecular Medicine at the University of Sheffield in 1991–2014. Duff was educated at Perth Academy, then a state grammar school in Perth, Scotland, and at Hipperholme Grammar

School, a school in Hipperholme, Yorkshire. He stu-died medicine at St Peter's College, Oxford, graduating with a Bachelor of Arts (BA) degree in 1969 and Bachelor of Medicine and Bachelor of Surgery (BM BCh) degrees in 1975. He undertook postgraduate research in neuropharmacology at St Thomas's Hospital Medical School, University of London, completing his PhD degree in 1980. His doctoral thesis was on body temperature regulation in rabbits. In 1975–1976, Duff was a house officer in medicine at St Thomas' Hospital, London, and in surgery at Stracathro Hospital, Angus, Scotland. In 2013–2014, Duff served as the Chairman of the Medicines and Healthcare Products Regulatory Agency. Since 1 July 2015, he has also been the Chair of the Biotechnology and Biological Sciences Research Council (BBSRC). In 2007, Duff was appointed a Knight Bachelor, "for services to public health", in recognition of his role in the inquiry into the conduct of a drugs trial at Northwick Park Hospital in 2006. In 1999, Duff was elected a Fellow of the Academy of Medical Sciences (FMedSci). In 2008, he was elected a Fellow of the Royal Society of Edinburgh (FRSE). In

2017, he was awarded an honorary degree by the University of Sheffield.

Punting in front of St Hilda's College.

Academic and Rowing Standing The Norrington Table ranked St Hilda's 26th on the 2006–2016 average, 29th in 2016 and 2017, rising to 13th in 2018. On the river, the first men's crew started at 48th out of 92 boats in Summer Eights 2018 and gained bumps every day. The first women's crew started at 32nd and was bumped twice. On points, St Hilda's stayed put at 33rd place out of 35 crews. But with a net negative of four bumps, it ranked 24th out of 34 crews.

ST HUGH'S COLLEGE

Highlights

- The fleurs-de-lys are for St Hugh of Avalon.
- St Hugh was a Carthusian monk.
- Henry II made him Bishop of Lincoln.
- Hugh successfully confronted Henry II.

Arms, Blazon *Azure a Saltire Ermine between four Fleurs-de-lys Or* (for St Hugh of Avalon).

Arms, Origin Attributed Arms for St Hugh of Avalon.

Arms, Meaning The stylized fleurs-de-lys (lilies) reference France, since the gold-on-blue (*or* on *azure*) is the mark of the French royal

family, and was used by Mary I, whose mother was Henry VIII's first wife, Catherine of Aragon. The connection of St Hugh's with France is that St Hugh of Avalon grew up in Burgundy, France. The ermine probably references Henry II's patronage of Hugh. The saltire may reference the martyrdom of Thomas Becket, for which Henry II of England was required by the Pope either to go on crusade or establish a Carthusian Charterhouse. Henry decided to do the latter and established a Carthusian monastery in Withan, settled by monks from the Grande Chartreuse. Henry invited Hugh to become Prior of this monastery.

Arms, Nominee—Hugh of Lincoln Known also as Hugh of Avalon, St Hugh is the best-known English saint after Thomas Becket, partly because of his fine biographer, a Benedictine monk of Eynsham named Adam, who was Hugh's chaplain and constant companion. The biography manuscript is in the Bodleian Library. Born in the Avalon château in 1140, Hugh at 15 joined a Benedictine monastery. At 25 he opted for the stricter life of the Carthusian monks at Grande Chartreuse. Henry II appointed him prior of a Carthusian monastery, the first in England, which was in the diocese of Lincoln. Hugh did well and Henry made him Bishop of Lincoln, then England's largest diocese. With great energy, Hugh raised efficiency in the diocese, protected Jewish residents, and gave special attention to poor and sick people, including lepers. Hugh kept up a friendship with Henry II, but disagreed with him. For example, he refused to provide a priest's living to one of Henry's courtiers, but managed the king's anger with diplomatic charm. He rebuilt Lincoln Cathedral, badly damaged by an earthquake, in the new Gothic style. He expanded St Mary Magdalen's Church in Oxford. Along with the Bishop of Salisbury, Hugh resisted Richard I's demand for 300 knights for a year's service in his French wars, leading the king to seize the revenue of both men. Hugh made several voyages to France on diplomatic missions for Kings Richard I and John. In 1199 the trip made him sick. He was able in 1200 to consecrate St Giles' Church, Oxford, but his illness got worse and he died later that year. He is buried in Lincoln Cathedral, was canonised by Pope Honorius III in 1220, and is today the patron saint of the sick, shoemakers . . . and swans!

Hugh's Swan On the Howard Piper Library stairs is a statue of St Hugh, probably placed there in 1936. He carries a model of Lincoln Cathedral in his right hand. His other hand rests the head of a swan, which is Hugh's primary emblem, referencing the story of the swan of Stow. The swan had a long friendship with the saint. Hugh loved all the animals in the monastery gardens, especially this wild swan that would eat from his hand and follow him about, guarding him while he slept and attacking anyone else who came near Hugh.

Founder The college was founded in 1886 by Elizabeth Wordsworth, great-niece of the poet William Wordsworth, to house women who could not pay the charges of existing colleges. Elizabeth used money left her by her father, Bishop of Lincoln, successor to St Hugh. Elizabeth is depicted in a statue on the library steps, wearing her doctoral robes.

19th century—Early Days The college opened at 25 Norham Road with six female students who were required to get the Principal's permission before visiting friends. The College gates were locked at 9pm. Rent was £18-£21 per term depending on the room size.

20th century—Main Building The main college building was constructed in 1914–1916 through a gift from Clara Evelyn Mordan, after whom the library was named. The college bought other nearby properties and received a Royal Charter in 1926. St Hugh's celebrated its 125th anniversary in 2011 with a summer garden party attended by 1,200 guests.

20th century—World War II At the outbreak of the war, the college site was requisitioned by the military for use as the Hospital for Head Injuries under the directorship of Hugh Cairns, the Professor of Surgery at Nuffield College. Brick huts were built on the college lawns with space for 300 beds. In 1940–1945, more than 13,000 servicemen and women were treated at the college. Advances in medicine made at the hospital reduced the mortality rate for brain-penetrating injuries from 90 percent to 9 percent. Staff and students were relocated to St Hilda's and other locations.

20th century—Coeducation St Hugh's accepted its first male students in its centenary year, 1986. In its 125th anniversary year, the college became a registered charity under the name "The Principal and Fellows of St Hugh's College in the University of Oxford".

Academic and Rowing Standing. The Norrington Table ranks St Hugh's 22nd on the 2006–2016 average, 22nd in 2016, 20th in 2017, and 28th in 2018. A new boathouse was opened in 1990, shared with St Anne's and Wadham Colleges. The St Hugh's men's first eight started at 23rd place in 2018 Eights Week and made a bump every day. The women's first eight started in 27th place and held its

position. On points, the overall ranking of the College began in 27th place and jumped to 22nd, an unusually large leap. On the 2018 net bumps ranking, St Hugh's was 4th out of 32 colleges and two PPHs!

St Hugh's boathouse.

ST JOHN'S COLLEGE

Highlights

- The coat of arms is that of Sir Thomas White, a Catholic.
- White was inspired by another Catholic, who founded Trinity.
- White was knighted by Mary I for leading her supporters.
- St John's ranks #1 on the Norrington Table in 2018.

Arms, Blazon *Gules on a Bordure Sable, eight Estoiles Or on a Canton Ermine, a Lion Rampant of the second in chief an Annulet of the third.*

Arms, Origin Granted to Sir Thomas White. Assumed by St John's.

Arms, Meaning Sir Thomas White had served as Lord Mayor of London. His arms as blazoned in Burkes *The General Armory* are exactly as used by St John's, although incorrect forms of the arms abound in published materials available today. The estoile usually signifies celestial nobility, which would reference Sir Thomas's

acts of generosity. The annulet is used as a mark of cadency for the fifth son, usually at the top of the shield below the bordure. The rampant lion on the canton signifies courage and strength, while the ermine implies royal patronage, which Sir Thomas clearly had since Mary I knighted him.

Arms, Issues The canton is sometimes shown incorrectly as *argent* instead of *ermine*. The *estoiles* are sometimes shown incorrectly with straight arms. The annulet is sometimes placed in the center of the shield. The bordure is sometimes shown incorrectly.

Nominee On 1 May 1555, Sir Thomas obtained a Royal Patent of Foundation to create a charitable institution for the education of students within the University of Oxford. Sir Thomas, a merchant tailor, named the new institution after St John the Baptist. St John was the patron saint of tailors because he made his own garments. His garb is described in the Bible as that of the prophets, a rough camel's-hair outer garment, secured at the waist with a leather belt (Matt 3:4, Mark 1:6). There is no heraldic reference to St John in the College's arms.

16th century—Sir Thomas White As a Roman Catholic, Sir Thomas intended that St John's would educate young Catholic men to be priests to support the Counter-Reformation under Mary I. The College's Catholic orientation is why Edmund Campion, the Jesuit Catholic martyr, studied at St John's. White was born in Reading, Berkshire, in 1492, son of a clothier. He was apprenticed, in 1504, to clothier Hugh Acton, who left him £100 upon his death, enabling Thomas to begin business for himself in 1523. White became master of the Merchant Taylor's Company and then Alderman of the City of London. He contributed £300 to Henry VIII for his war against Scotland. By 1547 he was Sheriff of London and sat on the commission for the trial of the "Nine-Day" Queen, Lady Jane Grey, and her adherents. White led the faction that supported the Roman Catholic side. Mary I repaid him by knighting him and then, a month later, insuring his election as Lord Mayor of London. In 1555, inspired by his friend and fellow Catholic Sir Thomas Pope, who had recently founded Trinity College, he obtained a royal license to found St. John's College, which he left £3,000 in his will. The College is dedicated to St John the Baptist. Sir Thomas utilized the buildings of the dissolved Cistercian College of St Bernard. In 1559 he purchased Gloucester Hall as a residence for a hundred scholars. In 1562 he suffered from a recession in the cloth trade and

died in 1567, a relatively poor man, although twice married. He is buried in St. John's College chapel. His legacy was astutely invested by his executor, Master of the Rolls Sir William Cordell, and during 1555–1577, additional gifts were made by his widow (they were childless) and others. With the failure of the Counter-Reformation, St John's became primarily a producer of Anglican clergymen and through the end of the reign of Elizabeth I the College's fellows lectured narrowly in dialectic, Greek and rhetoric.

Entrance to St John's. College arms top right.

17th–18th century—Feeder Schools White established a number of educational foundations that provided closed scholarships, facilitating the flow of students from the Merchant Taylor's School and five other favored schools to the College. This closed channel persisted until the late 20th century.

19th century—Endowment and Academic Specialties St John's was relatively well endowed by the end of the reign of Elizabeth I in 1603. By the second half of the nineteenth century the St John's investments in real estate benefited from the growth of the city of Oxford. The College's endowment became the most valuable of the Oxford colleges, as it included the Oxford Playhouse building and the Millwall Football Club training ground. The College gained a reputation for students pursuing degrees in law, medicine and the program of Philosophy, Politics and Economics.

Current Head of House The President since 2012 is Margaret Jean ("Maggie") Snowling CBE FBA FMedSci, a British psychologist. She completed her PhD at University College London. Professor Snowling is a fellow of the British Academy and of the Academy of Medical Sciences. Her contributions to the study of dyslexia have been recognised with the Lady Radnor Prize of Dyslexia Action in 2013 and other awards. Snowling was appointed Commander of the Order of the British Empire (CBE) in the 2016 Birthday Honours for services to science and the understanding of dyslexia. She has heavily promoted the "2000 Women" events to celebrate the 2000 women who have matriculated at the College since 1979, when the first female students were admitted to the College. (Elizabeth Fallaize was appointed as the first female fellow in 1990.)

Academic and Bumps Standing The Norrington Table ranks St John's 4th on the 2006–16 average, 12th in 2016, 6th in 2017, and #1 in 2018. In Summer Eights, the first men's eight started at 20th place and was bumped each one of the four days. The women's first boat, however, held its own in 10th place. On points, the four crews put into the water by the College dropped by one place from 15th to 16th. On bumps, St John's ranked 30th out of 35 colleges and PPHs.

ST PETER'S COLLEGE

Highlights

- College founded 1992 by Bishop Francis James Chavasse.
- The *dexter* side is for St Peter, the other side for the bishop.
- The bishop's son Christopher became St Peter's first Master.
- Christopher's twin brother won two VCs in World War I.

Arms, Blazon *Per pale Vert and Argent dexter two Keys in saltire Or surmounted by a triple towered Castle of the second masoned Sable sinister a Cross Gules surmounted by a Mitre of the third between four Martlets Sable the whole within a bordure Or.*

Arms, Origin Original Grant of Arms 19 December 1929. St. Peter's Hall was granted arms, in the year it was founded, on 19 December 1929. In 1947 St. Peter's Hall was given the full privileges of a College as a "New Foundation" and the name has been St Peter's College since 1961.

Arms, Meaning The coat of arms impales the arms of the Church of St Peter-le-Bailey, now the college chapel, with the arms of the founder, Bishop Chavasse. It includes devices representing: (1) On the left (green) half, *dexter* from the perspective of the shield-holder, are the arms of the church of St Peter-le-Bailey, i.e., the crossed keys of St Peter and the superimposed bailey or castle fortification. This church became the St Peter's chapel. (2) On the other (*sinister*) half, the four martlets around the English St George's red cross and the bishop's miter signify the personal arms of founder Bishop Francis James Chavasse. A martlet is a footless bird and symbolizes the endless quest of scholarship (the birds don't have legs to land on).

Founder St Peter's College was founded as St Peter's Hall in 1929 by Bishop Francis James Chavasse (1846–1928) and his son Christopher Maude Chavasse (1884–1962), later bishop of Rochester. They were concerned to provide a home for students of moderate means. Bishop Francis Chavasse dreamed of a new Oxford hall that would seek out eligible young men from poor circumstances. The dream was realized the year after the Bishop's death.

The Four Chavasse Sons. Bishop Francis Chavasse's son Christopher became the first Master of St Peter's; Christopher was awarded the Military Cross in World War I. Christopher's twin brother Noel was the only person in World War I to earn the Victoria Cross twice, the second time posthumously, and has been described as "Oxford's greatest military hero in the 20th century."

Noel and Christopher matriculated at Trinity College, Oxford in 1904 or 1905 and competed in sports (rugby and athletics) for the University; both ran for Britain in the Olympics. The 1920 Oxford University Roll of Service included the names of 820 Trinity men who served in the Great War. Of them, 153 (nearly one-fifth), died serving their country. Of the four Chavasse brothers, two were killed in action in World War I:

One of two stone memorials to Noel Chavasse.

- **Capt Noel Chavasse** was in the medical corps, treating injured soldiers, and for his bravery in August 1916 in Guillemot, Noel was awarded his first Victoria Cross, the highest military honor. He won a second VC in a battle in Belgium that killed him in 1917. He is the only soldier in World War I

to win a second VC ("with Bar"). He is also only one of three soldiers ever to have won the VC with bar and the only Oxford alumnus. He is buried in Belgium.

Noel Chavasse.

- **Rev Christopher Chavasse** was an Army chaplain wounded at Cambrai in 1917, and was, as mentioned, awarded the MC.

- **Capt Francis Bernard Chavasse**, also a medic with the RAMC, was wounded at Hooge and was awarded the MC. Francis became the first Master of St Peter's in 1929 and co-founder with his father of St. Peter's Hall (later College).

- **Lt Aidan Chavasse,** the youngest brother, also served with the 11th Battalion of the King's Liverpool regiment, renowned for undertaking dangerous missions. His Brigade-Major considered him the bravest man under his command. He was wounded on a mission to inspect German wire near Sanctuary Wood in July 1917. He sent his patrol back to safety and took cover in a shell hole. His body was never found.

2016–Centennial Events. In total, the four Chavasse boys were awarded 21 medals for their actions during WWI. Their two sisters, Marjorie and May, served as volunteer nurses at soldiers' hospitals. Several centennial events celebrated the bravery of the Chavasse family, and Noel in particular, along with an exhibition at the west end of the St Peter's College Chapel. In May 2016, General Sir Nicholas Houghton, then Chief of the Defence Staff, and a St Peter's alumnus and Honorary Fellow, spoke about Noel Chavasse. On October 13, 2016, broadcaster and author Jeremy Paxman delivered the second Chavasse memorial lecture at the Sheldonian Theatre before an audience of hundreds, including descendants of the Chavasse family. He spoke on "World War I: The War to End War", reminding his audience of the daily horrors of trench warfare and the sequence of events that led to it. He answered questions from the Master, Mark Damazer CBE, and members of the audience. On October 23, 2016, a ceremony at St Peter's College Chapel, at one time the church of St Peter-le-Bailey, commemorated Noel Chavasse's two Victoria Crosses. The Chapel was where the twins were baptized. The service, conducted by the chaplains of St Peter's and Trinity, combined the two college chapel choirs to number about 40, producing a reported "glorious sound". The service concluded with the famed quatrain of Laurence Binyon (Trinity 1888), "They shall not grow old", set to music by 13-year-old Zachary Roberts.

Current Head of House The Master of St Peters since 2011 is Mark David Damazer, CBE, former controller of BBC Radio 4 and BBC Radio 7. Educated at Haberdashers' Aske's Boys' School in Elstree, Hertfordshire, he attended Gonville and Caius College at Cambridge, where he earned a double starred first in History in 1977. He was awarded a Harkness Fellowship at Harvard's Kennedy School of Government, then returned to

England in 1980 to train at ITN. He became Assistant Director of BBC News from 1999, Deputy Director from 2001, and Controller of Radio 4 and BBC7 from 2004. He is a Fellow of The Radio Academy. Damazer has served on the boards of trustees of the Institute of Contemporary British History. He is the Senior Non-Executive Trustee of the Victoria and Albert Museum and a Trustee of the BBC. In 2013 Damazer captained the winning team on *Christmas University Challenge*, representing Gonville & Caius College, Cambridge. Damazer met his wife Rosemary Morgan at Harvard. He was appointed Commander of the Order of the British Empire (CBE) in 2011 for services to broadcasting.

St Peter's boat in Summer Eights.

Academic and Bumps Standings The Norrington Table ranked St Peter's 27th on its 2006–16 average. The College ranked 30th out of 35 colleges and PPHs in 2016, 28th out of 30 colleges in 2017, and 16th out of 30 colleges in 2018. In 2018 Summer Eights, the St Peter's first eight started at 33rd and fell to 34th. The first women's eight fell from 33rd to 35th. On points, St Peter's fell from 31st out of 35 colleges and PPHs to 32nd. On bumps, filling three boats, St Peter's came in 22nd, as the St Peter's second men's eight scored a bump.

ST STEPHEN'S HOUSE

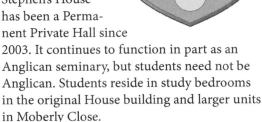

Arms, Blazon *Gules a Celestial Crown between three Bezants Or on a Chief Sable an apostolic Eagle between two Crosses crosslet Or.*

Arms, Origin Assumed.

Arms, Meaning Red for England, crosses crosslet and eagle (nicknamed the duck when used on a lectern) for the Church of England. The crown for Stephen (meaning wreath or crown in Greek), and bezants probably for the stones that martyred him after a trial by a Sanhedrin, a Jewish tribunal. The House motto in the full achievement is *Video caelos apertos* ("I see the heavens opened"), which were St Stephen's words, from *Acts* 7:56.

19th century St Stephen's House was founded in 1876 as an Anglican study center by the Tractarians (the Oxford Movement), whose leaders included John Keble, Edward Bouverie Pusey and John Henry Newman (later to convert to Roman Catholicism). The founder of the House was Edward King, then Regius Professor of Pastoral Theology at Oxford and later Bishop of Lincoln. Supporters at Oxford included William Bright, Edwin Palmer, Edward Talbot (first Warden of Keble College, who promoted higher education for women and is honored in the coat of arms of Lady Margaret Hall), Edward Woollcoombe, and John Wordsworth. In its earliest years, the House was situated on land where Oxford's Weston Library now stands. The first Principal was Robert Moberly, resident in 1876–88. All St Stephen's House Principals have been Anglican priests.

20th century From 1919, the House, nicknamed Staggers, had a site in Norham Gardens, near to the University Parks. In 1980 it moved to the current site, formerly the mother house of the Society of St John the Evangelist (the Cowley Fathers), across Magdalen Bridge near the University's Iffley Road Sports Complex.

21st century St Stephen's House has been a Permanent Private Hall since 2003. It continues to function in part as an Anglican seminary, but students need not be Anglican. Students reside in study bedrooms in the original House building and larger units in Moberly Close.

Current Head of House The Principal since 2006 is The Revd Canon Dr Robin Ward, former vicar of the parish of St John the Baptist, Sevenoaks and honorary canon theologian of Rochester Cathedral. A graduate of Magdalen, Oxford, he trained for the priesthood at the House. He earned a PhD from Kings College London, with a thesis on The Schism at Antioch.

St Stephen's House.

Academic and Bumps Standing St Stephen's House ranked 36th on the 2006–16 Norrington Table average, 25th in 2016 and 19th out of 35 in 2017, a rising trend. It was fourth out of six PPHs in 2018. Ripon Cuddesdon is listed as a PPH in place of Campion Hall, which does not have undergraduates taking examinations. St Stephen's does not compete under its own name in Summer Eights, but St Stephen's students (a boatload worth) were in 2017 permitted to row with the two St Benet's boats. In 2018 the men's eight held its own at 55th place out of 92, but the women's eight had a weak year in 2018, with five bumps knocking it from 73rd place to 78th out of 79, ahead only of the St Hugh's second women's eight.

TRINITY COLLEGE

Highlights

- Founded to fill the buildings of dissolved Durham College.
- Dissolution of monasteries supervised by Trinity founder.
- Arms are of the founder, Catholic Sir Thomas Pope.

Arms, Blazon *Per pale Or and Azure on a Chevron between three Griffins' heads erased four Fleurs-de-lys all counterchanged* (for Pope).

Arms, Origin ("Counter-changed" means the tinctures and metals are reversed. It is a translation of the Latin *transmutatus* and the French *de l'un en l'autre*.) Patent granted by Sir Christopher Barker, Garter King of Arms, June 26, 1535: *Party per pale or and azure on a cheveron between three gryphons heads erased four fleur de lys all counthercharged*. The following year, October 15, 1536, "he [Thomas Pope] was knighted by Henry eighth, amid the solemnities attending the creations of the earl of Southampton, and the gallant Edward Seymour, earl of Hertford, afterwards the famous duke of Somerset."

Arms, Full Achievement: The full achievement of arms includes two blue (*azure*) and gold (*or*) griffins as a crest on a crown.

Arms, Nominee Although the College is named after the Holy Trinity, the arms are those of Sir Thomas Pope, a Hertfordshire man who shared his arms with the college at its foundation in 1555. He asked for daily prayers in perpetuity, a request honored since. The arms are on his tomb in the College Chapel. The Pope family griffins survive through the College.

13th–16th centuries—Benedictines Durham College was founded in c. 1286 for the Benedictine monks of Durham Abbey. In 1544 it was suppressed following Henry VIII's break with Rome. Eleven years later, almost as soon as Mary Tudor took the throne, Sir Thomas purchased the old Durham property and founded on it Trinity College. Sir Thomas, a Roman Catholic, asked future generations of students to pray for his soul daily, since he was childless and wanted to be remembered, and probably also to make amends for having enriched himself as manager of the takeover and sale of monastic properties.

17th century—Durham Legacy The old buildings of Durham College are now clustered around what is called Trinity's Durham Quad. The Old Library at Trinity has windows from the Durham College Chapel, including one showing the coat of arms of an ancestor of George Washington. The current Trinity Chapel was built in 1691 in the presidency of Dr Bathurst; the carvings by Grinling Gibbons have recently been restored using the highest standards.

17th century—Lords Baltimore Both of the first two Lords Baltimore were alumni of Trinity College. The City of Baltimore, Maryland, is named after Cecil Calvert (1605–1675), 2nd

Lord Baltimore. Cecil's brother Leonard, also a Trinity alumnus, became the first Governor of Maryland. The name of the Baltimore Orioles baseball team came from the black (*sable*) and gold (*or*) colors in the coat of arms of George Calvert, First Lord Baltimore, which Maryland adopted as its state arms. Maryland is the only state to have adopted arms from British heraldry.

18th century—Three Prime Ministers Spencer Compton (1st Earl of Wilmington), William Pitt (1st Earl of Chatham) and Frederick North (2nd Earl of Guilford) were all Trinity alumni and prime ministers. Pitt made it safe for the colonies to revolt by chasing out the French, and North's statements and actions made revolt inevitable.

Trinity College, front gate.

19th century—Ecumenical Trinity's chapel services have been Anglican since Elizabeth I, but perhaps because the College's founder was Roman Catholic, it has been ecumenical. Two prominent Trinity Anglicans became Roman Catholic converts and were made Honorary Fellows of the Senior Common Room–John Henry Newman (the first Honorary Fellow, in 1877) and Ronald Knox. Newman was a student at Trinity and became a key figure in the Oxford Movement until his conversion to Rome, when the Pope made him a Cardinal but urged him to leave Oxford. Ronald Knox was appointed Trinity's (Anglican) chaplain during the presidency of Herbert Blakiston. When students went off as soldiers in World War I, student enrollment plummeted and Knox taught at Shrewsbury School. He converted to Rome and returned to Oxford as Catholic Chaplain at Oxford's Newman Center.

20th century—the Chavasse Twins in WWI. As described under St Peter's College, Noel and Christopher Chavasse matriculated at Trinity in 1904 or 1905. Noel was a medic and went on to earn two Victoria Crosses in World War I, the second one posthumously. Christopher also won medals and became the first Master of St Peter's College. On February 2, 2017, at Trinity College, Professor Mark Harrison, Professor of the History of Medicine and Director of the Wellcome Unit for the History of Medicine, gave a talk to commemorate Noel Chavasse's work, "Part of the Family—the Medical Officer on the Western Front." A bronze of Noel Chavasse dragging a wounded soldier from no-man's land is placed outside the Trinity College library entrance, with a bust of Chavasse inside the library and his portrait in the Chavasse Suite on Staircase 16.

20th century—What Would Gatsby Have Found? One famous self-proclaimed but dubious alumnus of Trinity College is a fictional character, the subject of *The Great Gatsby*. A real Trinity alumnus tried to imagine what it would have been like if Gatsby had actually gone to Trinity after World War I with all the clues in the novel left by F. Scott Fitzgerald. Famed Trinity alumni writers include: Viscount Bryce (*The American Commonwealth*), Lord Clark (*Civilisation*) and Q (Sir Arthur Quiller-Couch).

20th century—Heraldic Notes Trinity College's former Senior Tutor, Michael Maclagan, was Richmond Herald of the College of Arms in 1980–89. The immediate past President of Trinity, Sir Ivor Roberts, a Welshman, was H.M. Ambassador to Italy. His granted coat of arms uses a Welsh motto *Bid ben, bid bond,* translated into Latin as *Fiat princeps, fiat pons*—"Be a leader, be a bridge."

Current Head of House The President since 2017 is Dame Hilary Boulding, DBE, the first woman to head the college. Boulding was educated at Heaton School, a state school in Newcastle-upon-Tyne, England. She studied music at St Hilda's College, Oxford, graduating with a BA degree. Boulding then worked for BBC Scotland, working as a television director and producer 1981–92. She moved to BBC Wales, where she was Head of Arts and Music, 1992–97. In 1997–99, she was Commissioning Editor, Music (Policy) at BBC Radio 3. In 1999, Boulding left the BBC to join the Arts Council England (as it was renamed in 2002) as Director of Music. In 2007, she was appointed the Principal of the Royal Welsh College of Music & Drama (RWCMD). On her watch she oversaw £22.5 million of development including the building of a 450-seat concert hall and a 160-seat theatre. In the 2017 Queen's Birthday Honours, Boulding was appointed a Dame Commander of the Order of the British Empire (DBE), for "services to education and culture in Wales".

Academic and Bumps Standing Trinity ranked among the top ten colleges on the Norrington Table for 2006–2016, and has retained that status since then. It was 5th in 2016 (when rival and larger Balliol was 8th), 9th in 2017 (when Balliol was 10th), and is 10th in 2018 (when Balliol is 9th). Trinity has had 13 men's head-of-river victories, the latest being in 1949. In 2018 Summer Eights, the first men's eight made bumps on three of the four days, and rose from 13th to 10th on the river ranking. The first women's eight was bumped three times and fell from 18th to 21st. On points, Trinity rose from 16th to 14th out of 35 colleges and PPHs. Overall on bumps, Trinity filled four boats and suffered a net minus-four, ranking 24th.

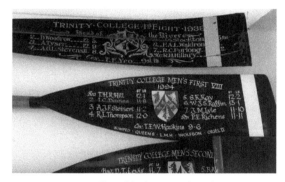

Trinity College blades in its boathouse.

UNIVERSITY COLLEGE

Highlights

- The arms with martlets are imputed to King Edward the Confessor.

- However, the college does not now claim him as founder, but rather William of Durham.

- It is one of the three oldest colleges at Oxford.

Arms, Blazon *Azure a Cross patonce between five Martlets Or (for King Alfred).*

Arms, Origin Attributed arms for King Alfred or King Edward the Confessor. University College's shield shows four (on its website), or often five, golden martlets around a cross on a blue (*azure*) field. University College has claimed the arms attributed to Edward the Confessor, the last of the significant Anglo-Saxon kings, although the founding in 1249 was by William of Durham, long after Edward. The College website says: "University College owes its origins to William of Durham, who died in 1249; however a legend grew up in the 1380s that we were actually founded even earlier, by King Alfred in 872, and, understandably enough, this became widely accepted as the truth. Nowadays, however, William of Durham is accepted as Univ's true founder, but that still gives us a claim to be the oldest college in Oxford or Cambridge." (The University College martlets are a possible origin of the four martlets in the St Peter's College coat of arms.)

Arms, Meaning The golden birds with no feet are martlets, symbolizing a ceaseless search for knowledge, as the lack of feet means that the birds cannot land. The University College ("Univ") coat of arms is imputed to their founder Edward the Confessor by later heraldists, since Anglo-Saxon kings had no coats of arms. The St Benet's shield includes an almost identical coat of arms on its top right (the *sinister side in chief*). The difference between the two crosses (Univ's is a cross *patonce*, while St Benet's is a cross *fleury*) is not significant, as both crosses have been used interchangeably in the posthumously attributed arms of Edward the Confessor. Edward was both a priest, hence the cross, and the last of the great Anglo-Saxon kings, whose death in 1066 precipitated a nine-month succession battle that culminated in the death of Harold Godwinson and victory of William, Duke of Normandy at Hastings.

13th century—Foundation The College was founded in 1249 by William of Durham. He bequeathed money to support ten or twelve masters of arts studying divinity, and a property which became known as Aula Universitatis (University Hall) was bought in 1253. This later date still allows the claim that Univ is the oldest of the Oxford colleges, although this is contested by Balliol College and Merton College. Blackfriars was founded before any of them, in 1221, but it is not a full college (it is a Permanent Private Hall), and its presence in Oxford had a gap of four centuries.

17th century—New Buildings Until the 16th century, the College was only open to students of theology. As it grew, the medieval buildings were replaced with the current Main Quadrangle. The foundation stone was placed in 1634, but the Civil War interrupted construction and it wasn't completed until 1676.

19th century—Screwing Shut the Dean's Door In May 1880, after an empowering Bumps Supper, some undergraduates decided to befuddle a Fellow, Albert Sidney Chavasse, by screwing his door to the frame. However, Chavasse had recently been appointed Senior Proctor by the University. The College authorities viewed the practical joke as an attack on the entire University. The Master therefore decided to send down (i.e., suspend) all of the students in the College until the person (or persons) who had done the deed came forward. Chavasse himself was the only Fellow who voted against this proposed punishment, being prepared to accept it as an exuberant prank. No one pleaded guilty, so the entire student body was required to decamp from the College that day. The young man who had screwed the door to its frame was Samuel Sandbach, but he had left Oxford for the summer in the early morning to attend a yeomanry camp and was unaware of the repercussions. When told of the College's action, he immediately confessed to the deed, and the students were allowed to return. The newspapers generally agreed that the prank might have gone too far, but the College was unjustified in meting out such Draconian punishment. A contemporary cartoon showed Albert Chavasse (cousin of the Bishop Chavasse who founded St Peter's College) climbing a ladder into his room through a window.

20th century—Coeducation University College became coeducational in 1979, having for more than seven centuries been an institution for men only.

Today As of 2016, the college had an estimated financial endowment of £115 million. Notable alumni include Bill Clinton, Stephen Hawking, C. S. Lewis, V. S. Naipaul and Percy Bysshe Shelley.

Head of House The Master of Univ since 2008 is Sir Ivor Martin Crewe, DL FAcSS. He is also President of the Academy of Social Sciences. Previously he was Vice-Chancellor of the University of Essex and a Professor in the Department of Government at Essex. Crewe was educated at Manchester Grammar School and Exeter College, Oxford, where he earned a first-class BA in PPE in 1966. In 1968 he received his MSc (Econ.) from the London School of Economics and Political Science. In 1971 he moved to a Lectureship in the Department of Government at the University of Essex. At Essex, Crewe was director of the ESRC Data Archive in 1974–1982, and co-director of the British Election Study in 1973–81. With David Rose, he established the British Household Panel Study and founded the Institute of Social and Economic Research at Essex in 1990. In 1977–92, Crewe undertook research on elections and voting behaviour in the 1970s-1990s. He argued that voters' identification with the Conservative and Labour Parties was weakening and that Labour was destined for electoral defeat unless it appealed to a wider social constituency. In 1995–2007, Crewe was Vice-Chancellor of the University of Essex. He was appointed Knight Bachelor in 2006. Named in his honour, the Ivor Crewe Lecture Hall at the University of Essex was completed in 2006.

Academic and Bump Standing The Norrington Table ranks Univ 14th on the 2006–16 average, 4th in 2016, 8th in 2017, 17th in 2018. The college owns the University College Boathouse, completed in 2007. In 2018 Summer Eights, the first men's eight started in 7th place and was bumped to 8th. The first women's eight was bumped from 4th place to 5th. On points, the five Univ crews together dropped from 6th to 7th place. On bumps, Univ ranked 10th with an average of 0.8 net bumps per crew.

University College, from High Street.

WADHAM COLLEGE

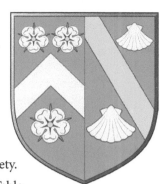

Highlights

- The impaled arms are for Sir Nicholas Wadham and wife Lady Dorothy (née Petre)
- The college was founded the year after Wadham died; his widow executed his will.
- A high point was under Warden Wilkins, a founder of the Royal Society.
- Wadham in 2018 returned to the top ten colleges in the Norrington Table, in 8th place.

Arms, Blazon *Gules a Chevron between three Roses Argent barbed and seeded proper (for Wadham) impaling Gules a Bend Or between two Escallops Argent (for Petre).*

Arms, Origin Ancient.

Arms, Meaning On the left-hand (dexter) half of the shield are the Wadham arms. On the right (*sinister*) side are the Petre arms, including two scallop shells, probably indicating that at least one Petre family ancestor completed the Via Santiago, the pilgrimage for St James to the great Cathedral of Santiago de Compostela. Dorothy, the daughter of Sir William Petre, married Sir Nicholas Wadham and founded the college. (Her brother was the first Baron Petre; the 18th was the author's contemporary at Trinity College, Oxford.)

Founder Wadham College was created in 1610 as a residence for men by the will of Sir Nicholas Wadham (1531–1609), from an old Devon and Somerset family. Lady Dorothy (née Petre) Wadham, like the widow of John Balliol, executed the will in 1610–1614. She gained royal and ecclesiastical support for the college, purchased a site, and appointed the architect (William Arnold). She drew up austere statutes that forbade any women from entering the college except a laundress of "such age, condition, and reputation as to be above suspicion"! The formidable Lady Dorothy appointed the first

Warden in 1613, Rev Robert Wright (a Trinity College, Oxford alumnus), but he resigned his office to marry before the year was out. Lady Dorothy also appointed the first Fellows, scholars and cook. Although she never set foot in the college, she kept a close watch on its finances until her death in 1618.

17th century—John Wilkins Rev. John Wilkins, Warden in 1648–1659, married Oliver Cromwell's youngest sister Robina (her first husband died). Wilkins, an alumnus of what became Hertford College, was part of a group of 50 men which met for some years in London to discuss the natural sciences. Many of the group followed him to Oxford and met regularly in the Warden's lodgings. The group included Robert Boyle, Robert Hooke, John Locke, William Petty, John Wallis, and Thomas Willis. Wadham provided twelve of the members, including Sir Christopher Wren. Those attending formed the nucleus of the founders of the Royal Society in 1662. The Warden's lodgings were crowded with ingenious instruments, and powerful telescopes were installed on the Wadham tower. Wilkins became the first president of the Royal Society provisional body and the first secretary of the Royal Society itself, which was the first champion of organised scientific research in Britain and probably in the world. He became a bishop under Cromwell, and during the Restoration, when his bishopric was taken from him, he became Secretary of the Royal Society.

17th century—Sir Christopher Wren Wren was an undergraduate at Wadham before he became a fellow of All Souls and astronomy professor at Gresham College, London. He returned to occupy rooms at Wadham while he was the Savilian Professor of Astronomy from 1661. Wren had notable achievements in mathematics, astronomy, physics and biology; his mathematical ability was ranked second only to Newton among his contemporaries; not till his 30s did he turn his mind to architecture.

Wadham College.

18th century—Holywell Music Room Wadham's Holywell Music Room is said to be the oldest room in Europe designed for musical performance. It was designed by Thomas Camplin, then Vice-Principal of St Edmund Hall, and opened in 1748. It contains the only surviving Donaldson organ.

18th century—Warden Thistlethwayte In 1739 the warden of Wadham, Robert Thistlethwayte, fled England after a homosexual scandal. The event prompted this limerick which may be the source of its apocryphal reputation for a relaxed attitude to homosexuality:

There once was a Warden of Wadham
Who approved of the folkways of Sodom,
For a man might, he said,
Have a very poor head
But be a fine Fellow at bottom.

20th century—Maurice Bowra Warden of the College in 1938–70, Bowra was committed to keeping the College open and meritocratic. He was known for his hospitality and wit, and the College has honored him with the naming after him of a new college building. Oxford colleges used to lock their gates overnight, and Wadham was regarded as a particularly difficult one to climb into after hours. One route into the College was via the Warden's Lodgings. By College legend, an undergraduate was sneaking through the lodgings when Warden Bowra entered. The panicked undergraduate hid behind a sofa, while Bowra took a book from the bookcase and read for several hours. When Bowra eventually rose to leave, he said loudly, "turn the lights off before you go, there's a good fellow".

20th century—Confrontation Averted In 1968, Wadham students joined in popular protests. They delivered to the Warden and Fellows a set of "non-negotiable demands". The Warden shot back the following widely reprinted response–

> Dear Gentlemen: We note your threat to take what you call "direct action" unless your demands are immediately met. We feel it is only sporting to remind you that our governing body includes three experts in chemical warfare, two ex-commandos skilled with dynamite and torturing prisoners, four qualified marksmen in both small arms and rifles, two ex-artillerymen, one holder of the Victoria Cross, four karate experts and a chaplain. The governing body has authorized me to tell you that we look forward with confidence to what you call a "confrontation", and I may say, with anticipation.

21st century—Gender, Racial Equality, Mandela In 1974 Wadham was among the first five all-male colleges at Oxford to become coeducational. The college has a reputation as a protector of gay rights. In 2011 it became the first Oxford college to fly the Rainbow Flag as part of "Queerfest", a celebration of sexual diversity and individuality. The Rainbow Flag also flies over Wadham during February, LGBT Month. Since 1987, student social events are concluded with the Mandela Freedom Song, a practice instituted when Simon Milner (1985), later

Policy Director at Facebook, was Student Union President. In 2017, the "Mandela-ing" tradition was challenged by a South African student active in equality campaigning. He made the case that the song was no longer needed after Mandela's release from prison and that Mandela's legacy was complex. A vote to remove the requirement to play the song after Bops was narrowly defeated in a Student Union meeting. In 2013 the Warden, Lord Macdonald, created the Wadham Human Rights Forum and he is quoted frequently in the media on legal rights and security issues.

21st century—Spreading the Admissions Net
Wadham is one of the largest colleges of the University of Oxford, with about 460 undergraduates and 180 graduate students. It has a relatively high proportion of state school students. Peter Thonemann, a Wadham classics fellow who also serves as tutor for access, said in May 2018: "We have among the highest proportions of students from the maintained sector of any Oxford college. We're also one of the academically top achieving Oxford colleges . . . We're drawing our undergraduate body from a wider social base. That drives standards up, it doesn't drive standards down." Wadham's admissions process includes an effort to reach areas where attending Oxford is not a typical expectation. The effort is led by specialists who seek out students in target areas such as Luton and east London boroughs.

Current Head of House The Warden of Wadham since 2012 is Kenneth Donald John Macdonald, Baron Macdonald of River Glaven, QC. He attended Bishop Wordsworth's School in Salisbury, Wiltshire. He read PPE at St Edmund Hall, Oxford in 1971–74, during which time he was convicted of supplying cannabis after mailing 0.1 g of the drug. He pleaded guilty and was fined £75. He was called to the Bar by the Inner Temple in 1978 and became a Queen's Counsel in 1997. He defended terrorist suspects (Provisional IRA, Middle East), major drug dealers and scam artists. In the late 1990s, he

was a co-founder of Matrix Chambers, specialising in human rights cases, with Cherie Booth and Tim Owen QC. In 2003 Macdonald was named Director of Public Prosecution, but was opposed by the Opposition party because of his business relationship with Booth, wife of then Prime Minister Tony Blair. The tabloid newspapers headlined his undergraduate cannabis conviction. Government officials responded that an independent board recommended the appointment. As DPP, Macdonald established the Counter Terrorism Division, the Organised Crime Division, the Special Crime Division and the Fraud Prosecution Service. He opposed a government attempt to extend pre-charge detention to 42 days. He was awarded a knighthood in 2007. Macdonald returned to private practice in 2008. The following year, he was appointed a Visiting Professor of Law at the London School of Economics. In 2010, he became a Deputy High Court Judge and a member of the Advisory Board of the Centre for Criminology at Oxford. In 2010, he was made a Liberal Democrat life peer, with the title of Baron Macdonald of River Glaven, of Cley-next-the-Sea, Norfolk. In 2010, Theresa May, then Home Secretary, invited Macdonald to review counter-terrorism and security powers. In 2011, Macdonald was named Chair of Reprieve, the international anti-death penalty and prisoners' rights organisation. In 1980 he married Linda Zuck, a television producer for Illuminations, based in Islington.

Academic and Bumps Standing The Norrington Table ranked Wadham 7th on its 2006–16 average, 6th in 2016, 13th in 2017, 8th in 2018. Wadham College Boat Club, the rowing club for students at Wadham, allows Harris Manchester College students to join. The college boat house is located on Boathouse Island. In 2018 Summer Eights, the first men's eight rose to 5th place from 6th, and the women's first eight fell to 2nd place from Head of the River. On points, Wadham fell from 5th to 6th place, within sight of Head of the River. On bumps, Wadham ranked 8th with seven net bumps on four boats.

WOLFSON COLLEGE

Highlights

- Founded by Russian immigrant who became wealthy from his mail-order business.
- Wolfson arms have a motto from Terence that embraces all of humanity.
- College's first leader was Sir Isaiah Berlin, another immigrant, from Latvia.
- Berlin sought to make Wolfson the most democratic of Oxford colleges.

Arms, Blazon *Per pale Gules and Or on a chevron between three roses two pears all counterchanged the roses barbed and seeded proper* (for Wolfson).

Arms, Origin The arms were designed *de novo* and not granted.

Arms, Meaning The pears indicate fruits of labor and peace; one source suggests the pears express the founder's gratitude for the end of World War II. The roses are probably for England. The Wolfson shield's motto *Humani Nil Alienum* means "Nothing about Humanity Is Foreign to Me" and is from the 25th line of the play by Terence (c185–159 BC), *Heauton Timorumenos*.

The Founder—Sir Isaac Wolfson Son of an immigrant to Glasgow from Bialystock, the shtetl made famous by *Fiddler on the Roof*, Isaac Wolfson built up Great Universal Stores to be the largest mail order company in Europe. He was made Baronet in 1962 and founded the graduate college in 1965 in response to an appeal from Sir Isaiah Berlin. Isaac Wolfson generously contributed to the foundation of the college. In recognition of his contribution, the college's name was changed from Iffley College to Wolfson College. He is the only person to found both an Oxford and a Cambridge College.

1960s First President—Sir Isaiah Berlin The liberal philosopher Sir Isaiah Berlin was the college's first president, and was instrumental not only in its founding, but establishing its tradition of academic excellence and egalitarianism. The college houses The Isaiah Berlin Literary Trust and the annual Isaiah Berlin Lecture. Sir Isaiah, the influential political philosopher and historian of ideas, was instrumental in the college's founding in 1965. He secured support from the Wolfson Foundation and Ford Foundation in 1966 to establish a separate site for the college, which included "Cherwell", the former residence of J.S. Haldane and his family, as well as new buildings around it. Installed in 1967, Berlin envisioned Wolfson as a centre of academic excellence yet with a strong egalitarian and democratic ethos–"new, untrammelled, and unpyramided". Berlin teamed up with his Vice-President, Michael Brock, formerly of Corpus Christi College, to shape the intellectual character of the college.

1970s Sir Isaiah's Egalitarian Vision Wolfson's main building was completed in 1974. Isaiah Berlin set out deliberately to make it the most egalitarian college at Oxford, reducing barriers between students and fellows by eliminating high table and providing only one common room for all members of the college. Academic gowns are worn only on special occasions. Students serve on the college's governing body and participate in General Meetings. The college owns land on both sides of the River Cherwell and installed a private footbridge to connect them. Its three quadrangles are named (1) the Berlin Quad after Isaiah Berlin, (2) the Tree Quad built around established trees, and (3) the River Quad into which the Cherwell has been diverted to form a punt harbour. The college owns the adjacent house and orchard, currently occupied by the Bishop of Oxford.

Today Wolfson College is now well-ensconced on the Cherwell in North Oxford, an all-graduate college with some 60 Fellows on the governing board, plus Research Fellows. Its interests range from the humanities to the social and natural sciences. The college is international and interdisciplinary, with students from 75 nationalities enrolled in masters and doctoral programs. It has been coeducational since its foundation in 1965.

Wolfson College.

Current Head of House The President of Wolfson since 2018 is Sir Timothy Mark Hitchens, KCVO, CMG. Hitchens was educated at Dulwich College in 1972–79. He

attended Christ's College, Cambridge, where he read English literature. After joining the Foreign and Commonwealth Office he studied Japanese and became Trade Secretary in Tokyo. Hitchens was Private Secretary to The Rt Hon Tristan Garel-Jones, Minister of State for Europe at the Foreign and Commonwealth Office 1990–93. He was speechwriter to the Foreign Secretary, The Rt Hon Douglas Hurd, in 1993–94. He was Head of the Political Section at the British Embassy in Islamabad, Pakistan, 1994–97. He was Assistant Private Secretary to the Queen, 1999–2002 and in 2005–08 was Deputy Ambassador at the British Embassy in Paris. In 2008, Hitchens was Director, European Political Affairs, in London. In 2010 he became Director Africa. Hitchens was appointed Companion of the Order of St Michael and St George (CMG) in 2012. In the same year, he was appointed HM Ambassador to Japan. Hitchens was appointed chief executive officer of the Commonwealth Summit in 2018.

Academic and Bumps Standing Wolfson is for graduate students only, so it is not in the Norrington Table. The first six places in the men's eights in 2018 were in alphabetical order at the start of Summer Eights, except for Wadham and Wolfson—Wolfson was in 5th place and was bumped by Wadham to 6th place. Wolfson's first women's eight did better, getting bumps on three of the four days and moving from 6th place to 3rd. Overall, on points, Wolfson rose from 4th to 3rd place. Egalitarian though Wolfson may wish be, its seven crews achieved 13 net bumps, which put it in first place on bumps.

WORCESTER COLLEGE

Highlights

- Arms are of Sir Thomas Cookes, a Worcestershire baronet
- He repurposed the dissolved Benedictine Gloucester College.
- It took half a century to build the new college facilities.
- Worcester benefits from ancient buildings and ample space.

Arms, Blazon *Argent two Chevronels Gules between six Martlets Sable (for Cookes).*

Arms, Origin Arms of Sir Thomas Cookes, Baronet of Norgrove and Bentley in Worcestershire. A bequest from Sir Thomas founded the college in 1714. However the Bromsgrove School, which he also founded, uses the arms with red (*gules*) martlets.

Arms, Meaning Your author and heraldic artist have a high regard for Marty the martlet. Unlike Larry the Bird, the martlet faces *dexter* on the shield. Twit faces the wrong direction, *sinister*, on a shield typically carried on the left arm. Marty the martlet is a bird without feet, signifying the never-resting search for truth of the intellectual. Marty bravely faces forward, toward the future or the enemy. Twit is running away, embarrassed by his limited vocabulary. Not a martlet by any stretch, rather, an embarrassment.

13th century—Predecessor, Gloucester College In 1283 the Benedictine Abbey of St Peter at Gloucester founded an Oxford house as a place of study for 13 monks. Over time, 15 other Benedictine Houses shared space, adding several lodgings.

16th and 17th centuries—Dissolution, Gloucester Hall Henry VIII's schism with Rome meant dissolution of the monasteries in and after 1539. The buildings remaining in Worcester from this period include the row of medieval "cottages" on the south side of the

main quad, Pump Quad and Staircases 1 and 2. In 1542 the College buildings were granted to Robert King, the first Bishop of Oxford, and he used them until he moved into the Bishop's Palace at St Aldate's. In 1560 the buildings were purchased by Sir Thomas White, the founder of St John's College, and they became Gloucester Hall. The penultimate Gloucester principal, Benjamin Woodroffe, attempted to establish a college for Greek Orthodox students to come to Oxford. It was a small but going concern in 1699–1705.

18th century—Refounded In 1714 the Hall was re-founded as Worcester College after a Worcestershire baronet, Sir Thomas Cookes, left £10,000 to create a new college. Building began in 1720. Lack of sufficient funds impeded progress but also saved the medieval cottages. The Hall and Chapel were completed in approximately 1770, using four major architects: Nicholas Hawksmoor, James Wyatt, Henry Keene and William Burges. In 1736, George Clarke generously left to the College his great collection of books and manuscripts. These included the papers of his father Sir William Clarke, of crucial importance for the history of England during the period of the Commonwealth and Protectorate, and a large proportion of the surviving drawings of Inigo Jones.

20th century—Coeducation Founded as a men's college, Worcester has been coeducational since 1979. In more recent years several new residential blocks for undergraduates and graduates have been added, thanks in part to a series of generous benefactions. Although

Worcester is near the centre of Oxford today, it was on the edge of the city in the eighteenth century. This has proved a benefit in the long run, since it has allowed the college to retain very extensive gardens and playing fields. The gardens have won numerous awards, including the Oxford in Bloom college award every time they have been entered for the competition. They are now managed by head gardener Simon Bagnall and a team of seven gardeners. A production of *Twelfth Night* was directed by Patrick Garland in the gardens with Oz Clarke as Sir Toby Belch and Francis Matthews. The college's gardeners keep a blog to provide an insight into the work involved in looking after the 26 acres.

21st century As of 2016, Worcester College had a financial endowment of £73 million. Notable alumni of the college include media mogul Rupert Murdoch, television producer-screenwriter Russell T Davies, US Supreme Court justice Elena Kagan, and novelist Richard Adams.

Current Head of House The Provost since 2011 is Andrew Jonathan Bate, CBE, FBA, FRSL. He is also Professor of English Literature at Oxford and Gresham Professor of Rhetoric and Honorary Fellow of Creativity at Warwick Business School. He has pioneered in ecocriticism, putting literature in a green, or environmental, context. He was educated at Sevenoaks School, St Catharine's College, Cambridge, and at Harvard, where he held a Harkness Fellowship. He was a Fellow of Trinity Hall, Cambridge and then King Alfred Professor of English Literature at Liverpool University, before becoming Professor of Shakespeare and Renaissance Literature at University of Warwick. His biography of John Clare (2003) won the Hawthornden Prize and the James Tait Black Memorial Prize (for biography). His book, *The Genius of Shakespeare* and his edition (with Eric Rasmussen), *Shakespeare's Complete Works,* published in 2007,

won awards. Bate's intellectual and contextual biography *Soul of the Age: The Life, Mind and World of William Shakespeare* (London, 2008) was runner-up for the PEN American Center's Weld Award for the year's best biography. His biography, *Ted Hughes: The Unauthorised Life*, was named by the Biographers' International Organization as an outstanding biography of the year. In 2006, he was appointed Commander of the Order of the British Empire (CBE) for services to higher education and was knighted in 2015 for services to literary scholarship and higher education. He was elected Fellow of the British Academy (FBA) in 1999 and Fellow of the Royal Society of Literature (FRSL) in 2004. He is married to author-biographer Paula Byrne.

Worcester College.

Academic and Bumps Standing The Norrington Table ranks Worcester 9th for the 20016–16 average, 9th in 2016, 4th in 2017, and 13th in 2018. In the 2018 Summer Eights, Worcester's first men's eight made four bumps, which brought them from 21st to 17th place and you would have thought would have led a major improvement in Worcester's overall place on the River. But the first women's eight was bumped four times and fell from 22nd to 26th place. Worcester's other two boats also suffered net bumps, so Worcester went up only one place, from 20th to 19th, on points. On bumps, Worcester's net negative of six bumps placed it 28th out of 35. A bump is a bump is a bump.

WYCLIFFE HALL

Highlights

- Named for John Wycliffe, leader of a popular movement.
- He and the Lollards were a precursor of the Reformation.
- Wycliffe Hall represented an evangelical response to the Tractarians.

Arms, Blazon *Gules an open Book proper the pages inscribed* VIA VERITAS VITA *in letters Sable on a Chief Azure three Crosses crosslet Argent in base an Estoile Or.*

Arms, Origin Created fresh and assumed.

Arms, Meaning The cross crosslets are for the Church of England. The red background below is for England. The book is the Bible and the legend on the Bible can be translated "The Way, the Truth, the Life." It is from John 14:6, and was spoken by Jesus Christ in reference to himself ("I am the Way, the Truth, and the Life"). The estoile may represent the evangelical spirit or divine guidance.

Wycliffe Hall arms in metal.

Arms, Nominee
John Wycliffe (often also spelled Wyclif) was a dissident priest during the 14th century. A precursor of the Reformation, he attacked the privileged status of the clergy and monks, veneration of saints' images, sacramental ceremonies, transubstantiation, and the Papacy. He advocated greater access of the public to the Bible, which in 1382 he translated from Jerome's 4th-century Latin Bible into the vernacular of his day. The vernacular Bible opened up a direct channel between the faithful and the word of God. Wycliffe's followers, known as Lollards (from the Dutch word *lollaerd*, meaning "mumbler") advocated a combined Christian and secular authority. Both Wycliffe (*post mortem*) and Jan Has (burned at the stake) were declared heretics by the Council of Constance, 1414–18, which reunited the Papacy but failed to make significant reforms, setting up Europe for the Reformation a century later.

19th century Founded in 1877, Wycliffe Hall was a reaction to High Church ecumenicism exemplified by the Tractarians or the Oxford Movement, which looked nostalgically at some Roman Catholic traditions rejected during the Reformation. But when Tractarian leader John Henry Newman in 1845 converted to Rome, many Anglicans recoiled. Those with an evangelical commitment, indebted to the insights of the earlier Evangelical Revival of the Wesleys and Whitefield sought to safeguard their heritage and train its future leaders. In its early years Wycliffe Hall was associated with evangelical leaders like former Principal Frank Chavasse (second Bishop of Liverpool, father of Double-VC Noel Chavasse), first Bishop of Liverpool J. C. Ryle, and former Principal Griffith Thomas.

20th century After steady growth over several generations, student numbers dropped dramatically in the 1960s as a result of Wycliffe's embracing a more liberal theological position during that decade. The situation was reversed with the appointment in 1970 of a new Principal upholding biblical orthodoxy.

21st century Wycliffe students and tutors in many years win top academic awards within the University and its alumni have experienced success as theologians, apologists and church leaders. Wycliffe accepts mature students (aged 21 and over) to study for the BA in Theology and Religion or the BA in Philosophy and Theology, very often with Senior Status—students who have already completed an undergraduate degree may start an Oxford undergraduate degree in its second year. Wycliffe offers courses leading to Christian ministry.

Current Head of House The Principal since 2013 has been Michael Lloyd, a Church of England priest, formerly the chaplain at Queen's College, Oxford and Director of Studies in Theology at Christ's College, Cambridge. Lloyd has published the popular introduction *Café Theology* and has a particular interest in the doctrine of evil and the problem of pain. He holds a BA in Theology from Durham University, graduating in 1983 with first-class honours. He also holds an MA from Cambridge and a DPhil from Oxford.

Academic and Bumps Standing In 2006–16, the average score of Wycliffe Hall on the Norrington Table placed it 31st, which was ahead of Regent's Park College (32nd) and all the other PPHs. In 2016 it ranked 26th but in 2012 and 2017 it ranked 1st if included in a combined Norrington Table (colleges and PPHs). In 2012 Wycliffe's five BA candidates all earned first-class degrees and in 2017 Wycliffe garnered five firsts and four upper seconds, with a Norrington Table score of a lofty 82.2. The problem is that the small institutions vary widely each year. In 2018, Wycliffe was back down at the bottom of the PPHs, although it would have been ahead of a couple of colleges. Wycliffe students wishing to row in Torpids and Summer Eights have applied to join the Queen's College boats. Queen's entered five boats in 2018 Summer Eights and ended with a net of one negative bump.

Wycliffe Hall arms on hat.

ACKNOWLEDGMENTS

The author thanks his wife of 48 happy years, Alice Tepper Marlin, for her important and insightful feedback on communicating the subject matter and language to the widest audience. Richard Lofthouse provided the *Oxford Today* platform in 2015 from which this book was launched. Paul Christopher Walton has been a true friend and valuable adviser since 2015, when he read the article in *Oxford Today*. Deep thanks to Lee Lumbley, the heraldic artist, and Jason Snyder, the book designer, for making this book look so good. The author has benefited over the years from the heraldry seminars at New York Biographical and Genealogical Society put together by John Shannon, who heads up the College of Arms Foundation in the United States. Although none of them is in any way responsible for remaining errors in this book, the author is grateful to William G. Hunt, former Windsor Herald; Elizabeth Roads, Snawdoun Herald and Lyon Clerk at the Court of the Lord Lyon; and Sir Henry Bedingfeld, formerly York Herald and Norroy and Ulster King of Arms, for their valuable guidance regarding details of British heraldry, for want of which the errors would have been more numerous.

The author and heraldic artist Lee Lumbley thank the following for their assistance and apologize for any inadvertently omitted names below, as well as for any other errors or omissions in this edition of the book:

Archivists and Librarians: Heraldry and genealogical sections of the Bodleian (Weston, Duke Humphrey's Libraries), the British Library, NY Public Library, Library of Congress, Society of Genealogists (London), NY Biographical and Genealogical Society, Oxford and Cambridge Club Library, London.

College Officers and Diocesan Clergy: Richard Allen, St Peter's College; Simon Bailey, Linacre College; Liz Baird, Wolfson College; Aimee Burlakova, St Antony's College; Sharon Cure, Trinity College; The Rev David Dadswell, the Diocese of Lincoln; Emma Goodrum, Worcester College; staff at Harris Manchester College; Clare Hopkins, Trinity College; Oliver Mahony, St. Hilda's College; Alice Roques, Hertford College; The Rev Adrian Smith, Diocese of Lincoln; Kristy Taylor, Green Templeton College; John Tiffany, PhD, St Cross College; Emma Walsh, Regent's Park College; Robin Ward, St Stephen's House.

Publishing Industry: Sheree Bykofsky and Janet Rosen; Mark Malatesta; Ellen Scordato, Stonesong Press; Susan Swalwell, Pavilion Books.

Readers: Thanks to readers of drafts of this book, especially Geoffrey Kingman-Sugars, Alice Tepper Marlin, Clifford Paice, Felicity Tholstrup, Paul Christopher Walton, and R. Maximilian Goepp III.

Members of Writing Groups: Poets and Writers, Harvard Club of New York City, especially Paula Brancato and DJV Murphy. Writers Collective, Amagansett, NY. Writers Window Pane, Indian River County Library, Vero Beach, Florida, especially TH Pine. Genealogical Writing Group, Indian River Genealogical Society, Vero Beach, Florida.

University Officers and Volunteers: Christine Fairchild, Director of Alumni Relations, Oxford University; Alex Galloway, President, and Cheryl-Lisa Hearne-McGuinness, Hon Sec, Oxford University Society, London Branch; Jonathan Ray, Public Affairs, Oxford University.

Website Authors and Managers: Thanks to the websites of Oxford University, the 38 Oxford colleges and the six Permanent Private Halls. Biographical information was obtained from these sites and other sources. Heraldry websites, especially Heraldry of the World, have also been helpful. Many people work hard to keep these sites updated; thanks to them all. This book's sources for facts, photographs, and artwork are credited and updated at https://bit.ly/2MTACMI.

HERALDIC GLOSSARY

The glossary was prepared by Lee Lumbley for use with this book.

Addorsed. Back to back, as in two keys with wards.

Annulet. A ring, also used as a mark of cadency (inheritance) of a fifth son.

Argent. Silver or White.

Attire. Describes a beast that has horns, such as a stag.

Azure. Blue.

Bailey. The defensive wall on the outer court of a castle or the court itself.

Balance. A pair of scales.

Bar. An Ordinary that spans the center of the field. Unlike a Fess, however, more than one may appear on the shield. Ought to be no more than ⅙ of the field and may not bear charges.

Barbed. The sepals of a Rose that appear between the petals.

Barry. A field evenly divided barwise by an even number. Unless otherwise stated, the shield is divided by eight.

Bendlet. A narrow version of a bend, permitting more than one but at the expense of the option to carry another charge. Example: Exeter College.

Beaked. With hard projecting jaws, of a bird or monster.

Bend. An Ordinary that spans diagonally from the dexter chief to the sinister base. Ought to be between ⅓ and ⅕ of the field and may bear charges.

Bezant. A golden circle or roundel, as in a coin.

Billet. A rectangle.

Blazon. The technical description, in words, of a Coat of Arms or other armorial device, such as Badge or Standard.

Bordure. Border.

Caboshed. Of a head facing front without a neck.

Cadency, Mark of. A device to difference a descendant (usually a son) of a living armiger.

Campion. *Silene dioica*, a bright red or bright pink flower with five heart-shaped petals.

Canting. Usually described as arms that use a "pun" but might be better defined as a visual display of a sound in the name of the founder or venerated individual. Example: Eagles for The Queen's College founder, Eglesfield.

Cantoned. Of a cross between four charges.

Charge. Any device borne upon the field, such as any beast, bird, or flora.

Chevron. An Ordinary that spans the field, issues from the base, and forms an inverted "V" shape. Whenever the design permits, the angle ought to be at 90 degrees. Ought to be between ⅓ and ⅕ of the field and may bear charges.

Chevronel. A diminutive of a Chevron. Ought to be no more than ⅙ of the field and may not bear charges.

Chief. An Ordinary that spans the top of the field. Ought to be between ⅓ to ⅕ of the field and may bear charges. May also refer to the topmost area of the shield.

Cinquefoil. A flowerlike device having five petals or leaves.

Cornish Chough. A thinner variety of crow that is black with red beak and feet.

Counterchanged. With colours inverted.

Couped. Cut cleanly, as in a straight line.

Cross. If an Ordinary cross, it is a division of the shield into four parts with vertical and horizontal lines that are usually of a different colour than the field, and wide enough to take a charge. If a charge, the cross is smaller and fits inside the shield.

Cross crosslet. A cross in which each limb also forms a cross.

Dancetty. A line of partition similar to *Indented* but usually with three indentations consisting of 90 degree angles.

Demi. The use of only the top half of a bisected charge.

Dexter. The left side.

Displayed. A bird's wings when they are spread with tips facing towards the chief, usually with the body of the bird facing affronty with the head facing dexter.

Edged. Of the edges of a book's pages.

Endorsed. See *Addorsed.*

Enfiled. Encircled by.

Engrailed. A line of partition that is a series of concave curves.

Enhanced. Usually of an Ordinary raised from its normal position.

Ensigned. Of a charge that is crowned by a coronet, crown, mitre, or the like.

Erased. Ripped roughly from rather than *Couped,* as in the head of a beast or monster.

Ermine. A small white-furred animal with a black tail or, more commonly, an Argent field with a stylised black tail.

Escallop. Sea shell.

Escutcheon. A shield.

Estoile. Unless otherwise noted, a six-pointed star with wavy limbs similar to a starfish.

Fess(e). An Ordinary that spans the horizonal center of the field and ought to be 1/3 to 1/5 of the field and may bear charges.

Field. The background tincture of and used interchangeably with the shield

Fitched or Fitchy. Normally of a cross where the base limb terminates in a point, also, when any charge has a point added to the base.

Flaunches. Arches on both sides of the field beginning along the base and terminating in the chief corners and always in pairs.

Fleur(s)-de-lis. Stylised lily, signifying French royalty or origin.

Flory. Terminating with the upper portions of a Fleur-de-lis, often used with crosses.

Fur. Includes *ermine* and *vair.*

Garnished. Adorned with or incidentally decorated by.

Griffin. A monster that is a combination of an Eagle with ears in the upper half and a Lion in the lower half.

Guardant. With the position of the head facing outwards.

Gules. Red.

Gyronny. A field of at least three wedge-shaped divisions issuing from the center point of a shield. When the number of divisions is unspecified, the default is eight.

Hilt. The handle of a sword, dagger, or knife. Unless otherwise specified, includes the guard. Examples are the hilted sword of St Paul crossed with the keys of St Peter in the Corpus Christi arms, and Plumer's sword in the St Anne's arms.

Impaling. A vertical bisection of the field with a unique set of Arms on each side. Often used to denote marriage or an official of an office, such as a member of the Clergy.

Indented. A line of partition similar to *Dancetty* but usually with five or more indentations consisting of 90 degree angles.

Interposed. Between and usually coming from the opposite direction.

Irradiated. Shown with beams of sunlight coming from behind.

Issuant. Proceeding from.

Lozenge. A square or near square set at a 45 degree angle.

Martlet. A small martin, like a swift or swallow, but invariably without legs or feet.

Masoned. Of the mortar of a wall or castle.

Metal. Gold (*or*), Silver (*argent*).

Mullet. A star. When the number of points is unspecified, the default is five.

Nebuly. A line of division of similar to a series of interlocking mushroom shapes.

Of the last. Of the first. Of the second. References to tinctures previously cited in a blazon. Increasingly, best practice is to repeat tinctures, to avoid confusion.

Or. Gold or yellow.

Ordinary. Basic geometrical design on a shield that divides it, such as a cross or a saltire.

Orle. Similar to a *Bordure* but detached from the edge of the field.

Pale. An Ordinary that spans the vertical center of the field, ought to be ⅓ to ⅕ of the field, and may bear charges.

Palewise. Vertically.

Passant. Of four-legged animals and monsters walking with the dexter fore-limb raised and the other three limbs standing.

Patonce. Of a cross where the limbs terminate in a slight three-pointed coronet shape as opposed to the larger *Flory*.

Paty or Patty (from French *patté*, like a paw). Of a cross where the limbs flare from the center point and terminate a wider straight line.

Pierced. A circular hole in a charge revealing the tincture below.

Plate. A silver circle or roundel.

Pommel. The knob at the base of a *Hilt* or handle of a sword, dagger, or knife.

Portcullis. The large grid gate of a castle or fortification.

Potent. Of a cross whose limbs terminate in a *Billet* perpendicular to the limbs.

Proper. As a charge appears in the natural world.

Purpure. Purple.

Quarter. One-fourth of a shield divided crosswise.

Rampant. An animal (especially a lion) standing on one hind foot, with forefeet and other hind foot in the air. Usually faces dexter, and has a straight raised tail.

Reversed. The opposite of the normal position, as in, *"in chevron reversed"* (Somerville).

Ring. See *Ward*.

Rod of Aesculapius or Asclepius. A single serpent wrapped around a rod.

Sable. Black.

Saltire. An Ordinary that spans the field diagonally from the chief corners to the base, ought to be ⅓ to ⅕ of the field, and may bear charges.

Slipped. The stylized stalk of a flower or leaf including trefoils, etc.

Stringed. Describes a feature of a horn in arms. Example: Coat of arms of Sutton in the sinister third of the Brasenose arms.

Surmounted. A charge that has another charge on top of it.

Talbot. Hunting dog.

Tierced. An equal three-way division of a shield, in this volume always palewise.

Tincture. Can be a colour (sable, gules, azure, vert, purpure), metal (argent, or), fur (ermine, vair).

Trippant. Of a deer in *Passant* position.

Unguled. Of the hooves of beasts or monsters when the tincture is different from the body.

Vert. Green.

Vulning. Pricking of the breast by the beak of birds so as to let drops of blood fall to feed the young.

Ward. The part of a traditional key that turns in a matching warded lock. The opposite end, held in the hand, is the *ring* or *bow*.

Wavy. A line of division that is a gently undulating line, often used to suggest water.

Map illustration © 2018 by Jonathan Addis. North is upper left, East is upper right.
The right-hand-side of this map corresponds to the bottom of the photo on pages 12–13.